The
Medieval
Longsword

This work was brought to you by
The School of European Swordsmanship
www.swordschool.com
And the patrons of this work who donated through Indiegogo and directly.

ISBN 978-952-68193-7-2 (hardback)
ISBN 978-952-68193-2-7 (paperback)
ISBN 978-952-68193-3-4 (PDF)
ISBN 978-952-68193-4-1 (EPUB)
ISBN 978-952-68193-5-8 (MOBI)

Book Design by Zebedee Design & Typesetting Services
(www.zebedeedesign.co.uk)

Printed by Lightning Source

Mastering the Art of Arms

Volume 2

The Medieval Longsword

Guy Windsor

For my parents, Roger and Maxine Windsor,
who have always supported my dreams.

CONTENTS

Introduction to the Mastering the Art of Arms Collection

In late 2009 I set out to write a longsword training manual to replace my first book, *The Swordsman's Companion*, which was published in 2004. Around that time, I had moved away from training and teaching Fiore's longsword material in isolation from the rest of the system, and had started to incorporate the dagger material into my "longsword" classes. So I wanted to put a chapter on dagger training into my new book. It was ready in its first draft by mid-2011, but it was clearly getting too big for a single volume. So I cut out the one longish chapter on the dagger, and some of the footwork and falling material, and wrote a separate dagger book, which was published in 2012 as *Mastering the Art of Arms Volume I: The Medieval Dagger*. About the same time it became apparent that the longsword book was still too big, so I carved off another volume, separating out the more advanced techniques and concepts.

While writing the dagger book, I wanted to point out that Fiore's original treatise was written in verse, and so took a small chunk of his text and laid it out as such. The rhyming scheme became immediately apparent. So I took the English translation and worked it into a sonnet; this spawned yet another volume, my *Armizare Vade Mecum* collection of mnemonic rhymes, published in November 2011. The frontispiece of this book, "The Sword", is taken from there.

What started as one book is now four: *The Armizare Vade Mecum, The Medieval Dagger, The Medieval Longsword* (this fine tome) and the provisionally titled *Longsword: Advanced Techniques and Concepts,* due out in 2016. This book and *The Medieval Dagger* are intended to work as stand-alone volumes, which necessitates some repetition of key actions and terminology. I have usually just copied sections such as "The Four Steps" from one book to another, pictures and all. In the advanced longsword book I have assumed a complete reading of this one, so that the fundamentals of the style are clear in your mind before we look at the really sophisticated material.

This book is intended to work with *The Medieval Dagger,* and to lay the groundwork for the next volume. I hope you find it useful and interesting.

Guy Windsor
Helsinki, April 2014

THE SWORD

I am the Sword, the King of Arms, Royal, Bold, and True,
All other arms will bend the knee to me when I pass through:

The cruel Lance, the mighty Axe, and the vicious Knife:
I fight them all, in vigour wax, bring misery and strife!

Enemies I shall constrain, and enter in the fray.
Challenge me and feel the pain: you'll wish you'd stayed away!

I'll take your Sword and throw you down, you'll think you were
in Hell,
The breaks and binds that are my Art, I do them all so well.

A Cross am I, the Royal Sword, Kings' and Princes' own,
And all who make a Cross with me, shall win their great Renown!

FOREWORD BY CHRISTIAN CAMERON

iore's *Il Fior di Battaglia* is one of the most important historical documents of the Later Middle Ages. If we cared nothing about swordsmanship, we'd still have to pay careful attention to the uniform quality of the art; the hundreds of illustrations, carefully drawn and almost certainly from life, showing men in various costumes at the turn of the fifteenth century. Approached differently, if we cared nothing about art or costume history, the information contained in the Getty Ms.. of *Il Fior di Battaglia* should revolutionise the way in which we frame the training of men-at-arms in the later Middle Ages; and through the revelations from Fiore's book, we can arrive at a much deeper, and very different understanding of what it took to be a knight on the battlefields of Europe—that is to say, in the world of Sir John Hawkwood and Luchino dal Verme, Bernabo Visconti and William Gold, Geoffrey Chaucer, the Black Prince, and the great knight, Geoffrey de Charny, all of whom were Fiore's contemporaries. Our picture of the Hundred Years War and even our perceptions of the tactics of medieval knights on battlefields, and in politics, too—should be drastically altered by understanding the commitment required to fully master the art of arms in 1400.

A modern soldier—even a soldier awaiting deployment to Afghanistan or Sudan or any of the far-flung places that Europe and North America have committed its sons and daughters—might profitably examine *Il Fior di Battaglia* for what it says about wearing armor and fighting in it; and for some practical grappling techniques and ways of thinking about combat that apply equally well whether your opponent is in armour or not. One of Fiore's basic principles is often *missing* in "modern" martial arts—the principle of absolute self-preservation. Every technique taught by Fiore keeps the user safe and covered while he kills his opponent or renders that opponent unable to continue the contest. Fiore's actions are *practical.*

I am a novelist, an historian, a former officer in the military, a re-enactor, a Medievalist and an avid, if amateur, swordsman. For me, *Il Fior di Battaglia* is *the* book. It informs me about cultural and costume history; it informs me as an historian on the practice of arms; it shows me as a re-enactor how to learn the whole range of chivalric weapons *the way they did* rather than the way we might imagine they did; it teaches me practical martial arts that I apply every day, and keeps me remarkably fit and healthy. It provides me with a window through which to view, not just a snapshot, but a whole documentary, on the life of a medieval man at arms.

There is a particular play that freezes the frame in time—that shows how deadly, and how practical, Fiore's art truly is—that informs me, as an historian and as a novelist, more than any other play, that this Master fought, that his art was used, and that he considered the most difficult issues facing his students in the list and on the battlefield, and that keeps me practising to reach the elusive goal of sparring success.

My favourite play is the play of the first master of the sword in armour and his two scholars. I'll leave it to Guy to teach the play— it's sufficient for me that Fiore first shows a cover—a parry; then he demonstrates an excellent attack from the parry—so first you make sure you are safe, and then you kill your opponent. But wait—there's more. Just as Fiore's work was being done—during the latter part of his lifetime—knights began to wear more and more plate armour, and most important, to wear steel visors over their faces. Open-faced bassinets were still common as late as 1400; many knights didn't wear visors.

But more and more did. And thus, our ever practical, profes- sional, and dedicated Maestro says "When I realise that my point can't reach the opponent's chest or face because of his visor, I remove his visor and thrust into his face." He illustrates just how to do it from the cover of the First Master of the Sword in Armour. It is essential to realise that this is a snapshot in medieval history—the moment at which men wore visors, but did not yet have catches and locks to hold them down. It is, in fact, 1380–1410. And that move—the cover, the brush of your left hand against the visor while you guide the point home to your opponent's face like a sharp making a pool-cue shot—and kill him instantly—speaks to me directly from across a six hundred year bridge. This was life and death. This was honour and preux and victory.

This is how it was.

In an ideal world, we would all understand the rudiments of martial arts, the essentials of bio- mechanics, and medieval Italian, and we would all read Fiore in the original language, leaf through the pictures, pick up a sword, and start practising. If, like me, you lack several of these skills, Guy's superb book lays out how to acquire the rudiments of knowledge of Fiore's art. I started with Guy's first book—*The Swordsman's Companion*. It absolutely is possible to learn the essentials of swordsmanship from a book. Especially this book. It is thorough, it is exacting, and it is beautifully written and very clear.

That said, Guy does not, and cannot, include in his book one essential element to your success as a swordsman. Commitment to practice.

Give it an hour a day, every day. And enjoy yourself.

Christian Cameron
Toronto 2011

INTRODUCTION

Welcome to the Art of Arms!

I make my living researching apparently out-dated skills and teaching them to the people who are interested in them. That, I assume, includes you. The sword has been largely obsolete as a sidearm for generations, and the style of swordsmanship you will learn from this book has been obsolete for about five hundred years. Half a millennium is a healthy distance from which to gather some perspective! So why bother? Simply put, there is no better way to develop yourself in mind, body and spirit than martial arts practice. There is no better way to understand your own culture than to study a different one, especially one from which your own has developed. And there is no better way to enjoy yourself than to engage in honourable tests of skill with your companions in the Art of Arms.

This is the perfect time to learn the Art. Now that our physical or social survival does not depend on it, we can study at leisure, with no hurry to gain the necessary skills, no need to focus only on the most combat-effective aspects, and absolutely no likelihood of having to kill or injure another person. Added to that, for the first time in hundreds of years, we have at least a good idea of how the knights of old actually fought. This is thanks to the discovery, bit by bit, of a huge treasure trove of manuscripts detailing the combat arts of the late Middle Ages. There is still very much to learn, but thanks to a decade or more of hard work by enthusiastic scholars all over the world, a good general picture has emerged. This book is intended to give you a solid grasp of the fundamentals of one medieval style, written down around

1410[1] by an Italian master, Fiore dei Liberi. His book, *il Fior di Battaglia*, is a staggeringly complete and detailed guide to knightly combat, on foot and on horseback, in armour and without.

Historical Martial Arts—What are we trying to accomplish, why, and how?

The practice of historical martial arts[2] is the process of recreating a combat system from period sources. As historical martial artists we make an act of faith: the writer of the source knew his art better than we do. It is often the case that the instructions presented in the manuscripts are obscure or counter-intuitive to modern readers. It is important to remember that for us, mistakes in training lead to a few bruises perhaps, and a lost match or two. For Fiore and his students, the consequences of an error could be death, disgrace, or ruin. With that kind of incentive, the chances are that when it comes to swordsmanship and knightly combat, the knights knew what they were doing. For pure historians, the point is moot. We do it by the book because we are engaged in recreating the historical art.

The process of recreating an art such as this begins with finding the source material you need. These days that's usually a simple matter—there are dozens of treatises available free online, dozens more reprinted in the last ten years, and many of the Italian, German and French sources have also been translated. From this cornucopia we select a primary focus—usually one book, which must then be studied in depth, read through many times, hunting

---

1   According to the Pisani-Dossi manuscript, he finished the work in February 1409. At this time the Julian calendar was in effect, which places the change of year on March 25th. By our modern, Gregorian calendar (instituted in 1582 by Pope Gregory XIII, and gradually adopted throughout Europe—the last country to do so was Greece, in 1923!) the year would have advanced to 1410 on January 1st, so we tend to date the manuscript to that year.

2   Some practitioners of Asian systems that have survived for centuries call their arts historical, because they have been maintained as faithfully as possible down the generations. I am using the term quite differently, and would describe their art as being from a living lineage. This is simply a matter of terminology, and does not imply any objection to other schools using the terms as they please.

down the meanings of obsolete words, putting together a sense of what the author was trying to say.

At the same time we must determine in what context the system is supposed to work—a fencing salle of the 19th century? A 17th-century battlefield? A 15th-century tournament? We then work through the book page by page, sword in hand. It is very unusual for a first attempt at a physical reconstruction to be even close to correct.

When working through the techniques in the book, we are trying to follow the text and pictures precisely, while fitting what we are doing into a broader tactical context. Often the author has chosen not to define his terms at all, nor to describe the overall tactical preferences of the system. This is a long, difficult, and demanding process, with many, many, sidetracks into error. I have found the only way through to be a combination of patience, persistence, and stubbornly holding onto the impossible goal of perfect interpretation and execution.

As we become more familiar with the source, we can hold more of it in our heads at once, and so make better and better choices in our interpretation. In short, the process looks like this:

- Find the book and read it
- Identify the context in which the system is supposed to work
- Go through and recreate all the techniques
- Identify patterns: recurring actions or ideas
- Identify the core style of movement
- Identify the core tactical preferences
- Train the techniques in a controlled environment
- Recreate the original context as closely as possible and try to apply the system there.

Once you have a working interpretation of a given source, and especially once you have taught that interpretation to hundreds of students, it is tempting just to leave it at that, and stop looking any further. This is death to the historical martial artist. Once you are "right", you stop learning. My particular path around this trap is to make it abundantly clear to all students from the start, and to you reading this, that as we learn more about these arts and the cultures from which they come, our understanding of how to bring the art to life will, and must, change. So do not invest in being right. Invest in getting *righter*. So long as the next insight actually improves and informs the art, accept it, change move on.

This will mean that you may spend a thousand hours or so doing something "right" that then becomes "wrong". The goalposts shift. It's not fair, but that's half the fun. You just knuckle down and spend another thousand hours getting the new material down. (To help with this I have included instruction on changing habits in on p. 50). This would be impossibly frustrating if I didn't have some kind of external compass to tell me whether the new material is actually an improvement over the old. Pure scholarship is not enough—there are plenty of more or less convincing theoretical readings of Fiore out there. My litmus test for a change to the interpretation goes like this:

- Does it match the text?
- Does it match the pictures (if any)?
- Does it fit with the overall tactical preferences of the system?
- Does it make sense given the specific combat context of the system?
- Does it work with sharp weapons at speed?
- Does it improve structure?
- Does it improve flow?

(Structure and Flow are explained in Chapter Two, *General Principles*)

If the answer to all of these questions is yes, I adopt the new interpretation. If not, I stick to the old interpretation, and keep looking. Some students do find this process of constant change frustrating, but it is really no different to the practice of any other academic discipline (how science has changed in the 18 years since I left university!) or indeed modern life (when was the last time you updated the software on your computer—or the hardware?). I have no doubt at all that Fiore himself constantly refined and improved his art. I only hope that the snapshot of it that we have revived is one of which he would approve.

My primary goal when training students is to prepare them for the duel. From a practical standpoint this is in a sense pointless, as duelling is illegal, immoral and very rare these days, but to my mind the likelihood of the context occurring does not affect the validity of training for it. We are engaged in historical swordsman-ship, not modern fencing using historical-looking equipment. For purely practical self-defence, most people reading this book ought to study nutrition, fitness, and advanced defensive driving. Be afraid of sugar, cigarettes, cars and alcohol: they are far more likely to kill you than someone with a sword.

My own research into medieval martial arts has focused almost entirely on Italian sources. This is thanks to an accident of educa-tion—I happened to study Latin, French, Italian and Spanish at school and University, so found myself able to read Fiore's work in its original language (with a lot of help from dictionaries and fellow scholars). There are translations available, which are extremely useful, but (for a professional at least) there is no substi-tute for working with the original text.

Before we get on to the specifics of Fiore's style, it may be useful to have a look at the breadth of material available for this period, which is mostly German and Italian. We have just a handful of Italian sources for medieval combat: there are four surviving copies of *il Fior di Battaglia* that we know of, and one copy of a later work by Filippo Vadi, *De Arte Gladiatoria Dimicandi*. The four surviving copies of Fiore's manuscripts are:

- *Il Fior di Battaglia* (**MS Ludwig XV13**), held in the J. P. Getty museum in Los Angeles. "The Getty", as it is generally known, covers wrestling, dagger, dagger against sword, longsword, sword in armour, pollax, spear, lance on horseback, sword on horseback and wrestling on horseback. The text includes detailed instructions for the plays. Regarding dating, in this manuscript Fiore mentions a duel between Galeazzo da Mantoa and Jean le Maingre (Boucicault), which we know took place in 1395. He does not mention Galeazzo's death, which occurred in 1406 (a crossbow bolt in the eye at Medolago). So it seems likely that the manuscript was written between 1395 and 1406. The treatise was published in facsimile by Massimo Malipiero in 2006, and a full translation into English was published by Tom Leoni in 2009.

- *Flos Duellatorum*, in private hands in Italy, but published in facsimile in 1902 by Francesco Novati. "The Novati" or "the Pisani-Dossi" follows more or less the same order and has more or less the same content as the Getty. The main differences are that the spear section comes between the dagger and the sword, and the dagger against sword material is at the end. The text is generally far less specific than in the Getty, but it is the only version that is dated by the author, who states that he is writing on February 10th 1409 (1410 by modern reckoning). He also states that he has been studying for 50 years, which would put his date of birth around 1350, assuming he began training at the usual age of 10 or 12.

- *Il Fior di Battaglia* (**Morgan MS M 383**), "The Morgan", held in the Pierpont Morgan museum in New York, proceeds more like a passage of arms: first comes mounted combat with lance, sword, and unarmed; then on foot, spear, sword in armour, sword out of armour, and sword against dagger. There is no wrestling or dagger combat shown except against a sword, though they are mentioned in the introduction. I conclude that the manuscript is incomplete. Most of the specific plays shown here are also in the Getty, and these have almost identical texts.

- *Florius de Arte Luctandi* (**MSS LATIN 11269**), recently discovered in the Bibliotheque Nationale Francaise in Paris, is probably a later copy. "Florius" has Latin text and is beautifully coloured. It follows the approximate order of the Morgan, though is more complete, containing all the sections seen in the Getty and the Novati.

It is much easier when dealing with multiple versions of the same source to pick one as your main focus and refer to the others when necessary. Most scholars working on Fiore agree that the Getty is the most useful source, since it is as complete as any other, and has the fuller, more explanatory, text.

The last of our medieval Italian sources, *De Arte Gladiatoria Dimicandi*, (Biblioteca Nazionale, Rome) was written between 1482 and 1487 by a Pisan master, Filippo Vadi. This book is a detailed discussion of swordsmanship theory, and contains illustrated plays with all the knightly weapons (sword, axe, spear and dagger). It shows a clear correlation with Fiore's art. One interesting difference is that Vadi includes a lot of theoretical discussion in his introduction, and very little actual instruction in the text supporting the pictures. This manuscript was published with text, pictures and translation, by Luca Porzio and Greg Mele in 2003, and my own transcription, translation, and commentary volume, *Veni VADI Vici*, was published in 2013.

The German sources are far more numerous, and present different versions of a system of combat attributed to one Johannes Liechtenauer.They include combat with the longsword, with and without armour; mounted combat; wrestling; and dagger techniques. This style was so successful in its time that the Marxbrüder, a fraternity of fencing masters teaching it, were granted a monopoly on the title "master of the longsword" in 1487 by Frederick III. This effectively made them a guild of instructors, and entitled anyone with the qualification to double pay for military service.

The Italian and German armoured combat material is very similar; the main difference lies in presentation. Fiore's art is set out in a clear and logical order, bound together by a common thread of guard positions, footwork, and a consistent tactical theory. The German system is presented far more haphazardly, with different sections often attributed to different authors. The two approaches are quite different in their usage of the longsword out of armour. German sources include an array of technical material that is absent from Fiore's art, and have some interesting omissions. It has been my experience that in terms of effectiveness, these systems are both excellent. High level practitioners of both arts can fence together as equals. I will cover the German material in more detail in volume three. For now, back to Fiore.

The Structure of *il Fior di Battaglia*

Il Fior di Battaglia is a vast and complex treatise, covering an enormous range of weapons combinations, techniques, counters, and fundamental concepts. As it was written around 1410, it comes from a different cultural and educational background from ours, one in which memory training was fundamental. As a result, the lack of theoretical discussion in the work, and the way the information is presented, can present stumbling blocks to the modern reader. The sheer amount of information is daunting, and as it is spread over some 90-odd sides of vellum (conventionally numbered 1 to 47 recto and verso[3]), keeping the structure clear in your head

---

3   These Latin terms are the technical names for the front and back surfaces of a page: the recto is the right-hand (usually odd- numbered) page in an open book, and the back of that page (which, when the page is turned, becomes the left-hand page, usually even-numbered) is the verso. Definition from The Columbia Guide to Standard American English (http:// www.bartleby.com/68/33/5033.html). Also it is worth noting that the pagination in general use and which I am using here is different to that employed by the Getty museum; because the first page has a "3" written into the corner, we number the treatise from page three onwards; the Getty numbers the pages from the first extant page. Malipiero gives both uses, the Getty's version in brackets.

as you read can be difficult, so I'll lay it out for you. The first three written sides (p. 3 recto and verso, p. 4 recto) are taken up with a text-only introduction. This covers the following points:

- A brief autobiography of Fiore himself
- A list of his more famous students and some of their feats of arms
- A brief discussion of the secret nature of the art, and Fiore's opinions about different modes of combat (fighting armoured in the lists versus fighting in arming doublets with sharp swords)
- A further description of Fiore's training, and his opinions regarding the necessity of books in general for mastering the art
- A connection of Fiore himself and the book with a higher authority (Nicolo, Marquis of Este) who commissioned the work
- An overview of the book and its didactic conventions, beginning with some background information on wrestling, and advice to the student on what is required
- Discussion of *poste* (the guard positions used in this art)
- A description of a crown and garter convention by which one can tell at a glance who is winning the fight in any given image.

This last is critically important to following what is going on in the treatise, so I'll expand on it here. The figures that begin each section are shown standing in guard, and wear a crown to indicate their masterly status. They are the "first masters". Following them are one or more "remedy masters" (also called the "second masters"), who illustrate a defence against an attack. Following each of them in turn are their scholars, who are identified by a garter, who execute the techniques that follow the previous master's remedy. After a scholar or master may come a "counter-remedy master" (the "third master"), wearing a crown and a garter, who illustrates the counter to that remedy, or to a specific scholar. Occasionally, there is a fourth master, who may be called the "counter-counter-remedy master", who wears the crown and garter too. Fiore specifies that most sequences don't get beyond the third master (i.e. the attack is met by the remedy, which the attacker counters), and it is perilous (perhaps because it is insecure) to go beyond three or four. This visual convention is unique to Fiore as far as we know, and makes it easy to be sure who is supposed to win from any illustrated position, and what stage of the fight (principle or guard; defence; counter to the defence; counter to the counter) is being shown. When reading the treatise, you can immediately identify who is winning in a given picture by his bling—the most bling wins!

The finish to the introduction is particularly interesting: "The colored letters, the illustrations and the plays will show you all the art clearly enough for you to understand it." In other words, this book should be enough to transmit the art completely. A bold claim, and one that is borne out I think, once the conventions are understood.

Weapon by Weapon: the Sections of the Manuscript

The manuscript is divided into sections, which are linked together. The primary divisions (mentioned in the title of the Pisani-Dossi) are on foot, on horseback, in armour and out of armour. The secondary divisions are by weapon. We begin on foot, out of armour:

- *Abrazare*: wrestling. This has one remedy master, and a total of twenty plays. The first sixteen are unarmed, then come two with a short stick (*bastoncello*), and two with the stick against the dagger, connecting us to
- Dagger: this is a huge section, with 76 plays, divided up

amongst nine remedy masters. This is followed by defence of the dagger against the sword, and hence

- Sword in one hand: this contains one remedy master followed by eleven plays, which will be detailed later in this book. They lead us to
- The sword in two hands: this starts with a description of footwork, then six different ways to hold and use the sword, then twelve guards. The plays are divided into
- *Zogho largo*, wide play: 20 plays, including two remedy masters
- *Zogho stretto*, close play: 23 plays deriving from a single remedy master, which is followed by
- Defence from sword guards on the left side—a single remedy master, with no scholars, who is followed by
- Staff and dagger against spear, and two clubs and a dagger against spear. This seems to finish the unarmoured material (though some of the dagger plays required armour). There follows
- The *segno* page, or "seven swords"; a memory map for the system as a whole, and illustrating the four virtues required for success in the Art.

From here on, we are mostly in armour:

- Sword in armour—six guard positions, one remedy master, one counter-remedy master, and a total of sixteen plays.
- Pollax—again six guard positions, eight plays with no specific remedy master, and two more showing variations on the axe: one with a weight on a rope, the other with a box of poison dust on the end. This is followed by the:
- Spear—first we see three guards on the right, one play and one counter-remedy, then three guards on the left, and one play.

And finally, mounted combat:

- Lance—five plays, each with their own master, including one counter-remedy,
- Lance against sword—five plays, including three counter-remedies.
- Sword—one guard position, shown against two attacks, with nine plays.
- Abrazare—seven plays including three counter-remedies.
- On foot with *ghiaverina*, a type of spear, against mounted opponents, one master followed by two plays.
- Lance and rope—a last play of lance against lance, showing a specific trick for dismounting an opponent.
- Sword against sword—a last, probably allegorical, play, in which you chase your opponent back to his castle, in which his villanous friends are waiting.

In this book we shall confine ourselves mostly to the three sections of the sword on foot, unarmoured. This does not suggest that these sections are somehow a standalone treatise; on the contrary, understanding them has required many readings of the entire manuscript, and exhaustive recreation of the entire system on foot. The sections complement and reinforce each other: when a longsword pommel strike comes in, treat it like a dagger attack: when you end up too close to use your pollax, use the wrestling plays. There is much to learn about the spear from the plays of the sword, and so on. I have left out the plays in armour simply because most readers will not have access to a complete harness, and there is no point doing armoured plays without it. Likewise, we should not imagine that the work is done: there remain (in other sections) plays that have not yet been convincingly interpreted by anyone, and the mounted combat material is beyond the scope of any but the very best riders, with highly trained horses.

In any given section there will usually be one or more "remedy masters" wearing a crown, illustrating the defence against a particular attack. These are followed by scholars, wearing a garter, who complete the play of the previous master. There are often also counter-remedy masters, wearing a crown and a garter, which counter either the scholar that comes before them, or the master himself. In other words their action may be specific to one scholar, or more generally applicable to the remedy itself.

The plays are the illustrations of the techniques, so a picture of a player (wearing no crown or garter) getting beaten by a master, scholar, or counter-remedy master. One technical sequence, such as a parry and strike, might take up one, two or three such illustrations, each of which is a play. As the term implies, there is often a lot of "play" in the execution of these techniques, and several different ways to enter into a given play. Fiore scholars tend to keep the key plays in memory, in the order that they appear in the Getty MS. It has become the norm to refer to the plays by their number—such as "the third play of the second master of *zogho largo*". This is more useful than saying "p. 25 verso, bottom left illustration", because it puts the play into its context. It is also how Fiore himself refers to the plays. In this numbering system, the illustration showing the master is the first play, and all the images that follow him, up to the next master, are numbered two, three, etc. This makes it very easy to find the play referred to—simply find the right master (wearing a crown and no garter), and count from there. So when reading this book, if you keep a copy of the treatise handy, you should be able to find the source for every technique I describe.

Context is King

Every martial art is a set of actions and choices designed to achieve victory in a specific martial context. What constitutes victory can vary hugely—from pinning someone down on their back for three seconds, to tapping them on the nose with your fist, to smashing them to a pulp with a huge axe, to blowing them up with a grenade. Or indeed, pushing them out of the ring, or stabbing them in the face with a sword. What works appropriately in one context may well fail miserably in another.

Question: who would win—a sniper or a boxer?

Answer: with gloves on in the ring, the boxer. At 1000 yards with rifles, the sniper. In a bar fight, who knows? But my money would be on the boxer, as a bar fight is closer in context to the ring than it is to shooting from far away. But then a sniper is trained to kill people, and the boxer isn't, so I wouldn't bet my house on it.

Of course, many arts are supposed to work in two or more environments, and have lethal and non- lethal responses that the practitioner should apply depending on circumstances. Perhaps the most obvious modern example of this is the armed police officer, who will generally carry a gun, pepper spray, and a night-stick, and is expected to use the correct weapon, or none, as the circumstance demands. The rowdy drunk who means no real harm but takes a swing at a cop gets treated differently from the armed robber coming out of a bank shooting. This to my mind requires a profound and sophisticated level of training.

So the first question we must ask ourselves when beginning the study of a new martial art is this: in what contexts is this art supposed to work? Fiore, thankfully, tells us of several:

- Combat with sharp swords in a gambeson (a thick padded jacket) and without any other defensive weapon besides a pair of chamois gloves. In this context, "a single failed parry can be fatal".
- In the lists, where "a combatant wearing good armour can receive multiple hits and still go on to win the fight". Also, often, neither combatant dies because one will hold the other to ransom; a common practice in this period. The lists are a formal, fenced off area for pre-arranged combat such as tournament play or the judicial duel.
- *Abrazare* (wrestling) which "is of two kinds: one is done for pleasure, the other in anger, or for one's life, employing every

trick, deception and cruelty imaginable".

It is clear then that combat can be done for pleasure or for "real", in armour or without, in the lists or outside them.

The judicial duel was considered by many in Fiore's time the highest expression of the art of arms, because in it, everything possible was done to make the combat equal. Luck was, as far as possible, not a deciding factor in the outcome. For example, in some cases if my sword broke by accident, the fight might stop and I would get a new one. If you deliberately broke my sword, the fight would continue. If you were to slip on a patch of mud, I might be obliged to stop and let you up; if I were to throw you to the ground I would get to take advantage of it. (And sometimes breaking your opponent's sword or successfully throwing them to the ground would grant you an automatic victory.)

One fascinating aspect of the judicial duel in Italy was the roles of challenger and challenged—the challenger was obliged by law to open the fight with a committed attack, and the challenged was equally obliged to await the attack. Hence Fiore's recommendations of specific guards being good to wait in, and the apparent absence in this system of the concept of initiative, which is a critical component of most other martial arts. Likewise, the challenged party was only obliged to withstand the duel. If he was still fighting when the sun went down, he would win by default. This would sometimes result in the challenger being executed.

The equipment required, such as weapons, armour, and horses was all determined beforehand. The duel could be on horseback or on foot, in armour or unarmoured, and with a huge variety of weapons. This explains in part why Fiore included such a range of material. It does not explain though why in many places in the book the combatants are unequally equipped—sword versus dagger, for instance. This may be just a pedagogical convention, connecting (in this example) the dagger material to the sword, but more likely in my opinion, the art is also expected to work in less formal engagements.

The primary contexts in which we know Fiore's art is supposed to work then are:

- The judicial duel
- The tournament
- The private duel.

And we may also surmise from the fact that unequally armed combatants are also depicted that it should be applicable in the following environments also:

- Battle
- Personal self-defence (in a 14th or 15th-century urban or rural environment).

At no point does Fiore explicitly discuss defence against multiple opponents, battle tactics, or self-defence, except perhaps where he shows a man with a short stick (*bastoncello*) defending himself against a dagger attack *while sitting down*! But the majority of the dagger plays depict an unarmed defender against an armed attacker, so we may assume his art is not only for the lists.

We cannot accurately reproduce any of these contexts in this day and age. Even if the equipment was perfect, the social pressures, prior conditioning and expectations, and of course the legality of public murder, are all completely different. But just about everyone involved in recreating these arts agrees that freeplay, where we try to win mock swordfights but do no harm, is a vitally important aspect of our practice. Where we differ is the role that freeplay (or fencing, or sparring, or bouting) occupies in our approach.

For many practitioners, freeplay *is* the purpose of their training—they practice simply to become good at it, according to whatever rules they decide. There is nothing wrong with this, but for those of us engaged in figuring out Fiore's art, we must first realize that freeplay as we do it does not in the least replicate the context for which Fiore's art was designed to work. There is just no way that freeplay can be as safe as our culture requires it to be, and yet adequately reproduce the physical and emotional conditions of actual combat. So we have a choice—either we use freeplay as just one more angle on training, or we adapt our training to become expert in our freeplay context. You can't really do both simultaneously, as the contexts are so far removed. Historical technique will often fail in freeplay, just as modern tournament freeplay would probably fail in knightly combat.

As I see it, a martial artist trains to be emotionally and physically capable of taking life in a righteous cause. A fencer trains to win fencing matches by scoring hits without doing injury. Between one pole (kill your enemies) and the other (fence to the rules) exists a huge range of fencing-like activities, with a more or less opaque wall thrown up between them: behind which, we train to kill; in front of which, we train not to. Deciding where on this continuum, and on which side of the wall, you wish to train, determines more than any other factor what part freeplay should play in your practice.

If we want our freeplay to improve our understanding of Fiore's art, we must replicate as closely as possible the context in which Fiore's art is supposed to work, *and be aware of the differences.* The primary difference is the intent of the combatants. I have students who have professional experience of mortal combat, such as police officers and soldiers. It has always surprised me that they'd train under me, as I have no actual experience of the context for which I am training them. But as one of them put it, he already knows about fighting, he's interested in *swords*, something he never sees at work. Fencing with him is really interesting, as I can quite easily control the match, and so long as the contest is friendly (i.e. no injuries intended), the outcome is pretty certain. But I am sure that if we flicked a mental switch and tried to kill each other, he'd take me apart—because he's trained and experienced in dealing with people trying to kill him. In my opinion, that factor outweighs all others, simply because the emotional context of mortal combat is (according to my research—remember, no experience) overwhelming, and until you are conditioned for it, it precludes the use of anything clever. This was well known back in the day, as the following quotation from dall' Agocchie illustrates; the treatise takes the form (as many do) of a conversation between peers (Lepido Ranieri and Giovanni dall' Agocchie):

> **Lep:** I rest with great satisfaction thereof, but certain doubts remain which I'd like you to clarify for me (before we move on), and one of them is this: there are many who say that when acting in earnest one can't perform the many subtleties as there are in this art.
>
> **Gio:** What do you mean by "subtleties"?
>
> **Lep:** They say that one can't feint, nor disengage, and that there isn't enough time to perform body evasions and similar things.
>
> **Gio:** They say this because one rarely finds men who aren't moved by wrath or fear or something else when it comes to acting in earnest, which causes their intellect to become clouded and for this reason they can't employ them. But I say to you that if they don't allow themselves to be defeated by these circumstances, and they keep their heads, although they may be difficult, they'll do them safely.
>
> **Lep.** But what's the reason for teaching them if they're so difficult to employ in earnest?
>
> **Gio:** They're taught so that courageous men can avail themselves of them in the appropriate occasions. Because one often sees many who were somewhat timid and fearful, yet nonetheless were able to perform them excellently when done in play; but then they were unable to avail themselves of them when the occasion arose in which to do them in earnest.
>
> **Lep:** I believe it, because when one loses spirit, one consequently loses art as well.

From: *On the Art of Fencing* (1572) pp. 32 recto and verso, translated
    by Jherek Swanger.

For this reason, I think that freeplay is a very unreliable indication
of *duelling* skill. One of the very few competitive fencers to actually
fight a duel, Aldo Nadi, put it like this: "I am more than ever
convinced that from a fencer's point of view, a duel is inconclusive.
His is a sport of skill—not of kill." (*The Living Sword*, pp151-152)

At the time of his encounter, Nadi was without doubt the best
fencer in the world, easily beating anyone he faced on the strip.
His opponent, the journalist Adolfo Cotronei, not much of a fencer
by any standard, struck first, wounding Nadi in the forearm. Nadi
rallied and wounded Cotronei in several places. It is well worth
reading Nadi's book for this chapter alone, as he describes in detail
the difference to him between top level sport fencing, and duelling
with a sharp version of the same weapon.

Our dilemma is that Fiore's art is primarily concerned with
earnest encounters, and employs actions that are primarily
supposed to work in that context—simple, brutal, and efficient.
Any freeplay context we create that does not include mortal fear
is going to encourage different actions.

Equipment is less important, but nonetheless has an effect. In
my experience, blunt steel swords of good quality are by far the
best tools for replicating Fiore's art in freeplay. Sharp steel would
be better, but it is unacceptably risky. Having established that we
are already sacrificing some authenticity for safety, the question
becomes: how far do you go? Some practitioners use aluminium,
even bamboo or plastic, but these tools behave so differently to
steel, and encourage so little honest fear, that they are in my opinion
worthless for historical swordsmanship. Much depends on the
available equipment and the training goals of the individual fencers,
clubs or schools involved, and far be it from me to tell you what
to do. Let me say at this point that freeplay is an essential part of
the recreation of the art, and is an excellent way for two fencers

to test their skills. Problems only arise when we mistake success in one context for success in another.

In this book I assume that your motivation is similar to mine—I am very much on the far side of the wall, and want to recreate Fiore's art as purely as possible. Once martial arts develop towards competitive sports my interest wanes. Bear my biases in mind when following the instructions.

A Word about Language

You will already have noticed several uses of Italian terms. In my opinion, it is best to use Fiore's own words as much as is practicable when training. This helps us to stay mindful of where our material is coming from, and acts as a starting point for students looking to work with the original source themselves. Compare the following:

"Strike with a forehand descending blow from the guard of the woman into long guard"
and
"Strike a *mandritto fendente* from *posta di donna* into *posta longa*"

To me, the second is infinitely preferable. It is more precise, as by using Fiore's terminology we are inherently referring to his way of doing the "forehand descending blow", and therefore everything that he wrote about that blow is automatically brought to bear. It evokes the time and culture from which this art descends. And finally it solves any possible translation errors by eliminating translation.

Using Fiore's terms is made a little harder by the fact that spelling was not yet standardized. Fiore will occasionally spell the same word three different ways in the same paragraph. In each case I have just picked my favourite and stuck with it. For example, *zogho* (play) is *gioco* in modern Italian; *zenghiaro* (boar)is now *chinghiale*. I have stuck with one of Fiore's spellings because again, it connects the interpretation of the action more precisely to this specific text.

Most of my readers are as yet unable to read Italian in any form (indeed, that's one of the reasons books like this are necessary) and so I have provided a glossary at the back of this book, and highlighted the meaning of every new term as it is introduced.

Something to be aware of though; using the original language for a term does tend to make it appear as a piece of technical jargon, which can be misleading. When Fiore wrote, for example, *accresco fora di strada*, it just means "I step out of the way". But put in Italian it feels much more specific. That precision is not inherent in the original language. So let's use his terms, but not read too much into them.

I understand that for most readers, learning these terms is a major undertaking. To make this easier, and to help you internalize the tactical structure of the system, I have developed a card game, *Audatia.* By playing this game you will naturally pick up the terminology, and learn what particular actions are good for, how you should strike from a particular guard, and so forth, without really thinking about it. I highly recommend it for all students of Fiore's Art. See www.audatiagame.com for details.

You Can't Learn Martial Arts from Reading a Book!

We hear this a lot, and it is *true*, but not *accurate*. People can and do. It is more accurate to say that you can't learn martial arts by only sitting down and reading a book. You have to practise the exercises, compare what you're doing with what's written, practise again, do more drills, test your skills against various feedback systems (hitting targets, sparring, etc.), then go back to the book and check again, then practise some more, and so on.

In his introduction, Fiore says that his student, Galeazzo da Mantova (a famous knight, and so something of an authority on combat), was of the opinion that "without books, nobody can truly be a Master or student in this art". Fiore goes on to say that "I, Fiore, agree with this: there is so much to this art that even the man with the keenest memory in the world will be unable to learn more than a fourth of it without books." The book thus serves as an aid to memory.

It is much more efficient for the student to have a proper instructor, but I can reach infinitely more students through a book than I can teach in person. One of the greatest benefits to me from writing my first book, *The Swordsman's Companion*, was the way it got many people started in medieval martial arts, many of whom used my book to start their own study groups (either completely independently or as part of my school). Even better, some began working with the original sources and emailed me to tell me where I'd got it wrong! So, as you start using this book, bear in mind that it is practically impossible that everything I write is correct, or that you will replicate every action exactly as I intend it. Keep your common sense filter engaged, keep your goals in mind, and enjoy the process.

I originally imagined this book as forming an overview of the art; detailing *all* the guard positions, then *all* the drills, then putting together a huge pile of drills for readers to work through. This is pretty much the standard model for books like this, and indeed is pretty close to the way most treatises are put together. However, I realized after completing the first draft that it is not the way I teach, and it is not the most natural way for most people trying to learn this material *as a living art* to pick up the core skills and theory. So, I have organised it more organically—first theory, because that exists outside practice anyway, then basic solo actions, creating basic positions, and basic pair drills, and adding actions, guard positions and drills as I would in class. For those readers looking for an overview, I have included a summary of the actions, guards, and techniques in the appendix "The System by Numbers".

Chapter One

TOOLS OF THE TRADE: NECESSARY EQUIPMENT FOR TRAINING IN THE ART OF ARMS

I do a lot of my practice without any equipment at all. But swordsmanship requires swords, and historical swordsmanship requires books and swords. This Art can be an expensive hobby, so don't feel that you need to splash out on everything right away. You can get started with just this book and a stick. But eventually, you will need more than one book, and more than one piece of equipment.

Books

The book you are holding is, I hope you will find, a good start in getting to grips with historical swordsmanship. It is, though, by no means the only book you should have in your library. As we saw in the introduction, Fiore himself believed that it was impossible to master the art without books. If your goals are simply to work through this book and get good at longsword fencing by doing everything I say in it, then skip this part and go straight to the rest of the equipment section. Those of you who are interested in furthering the art by your own research, but are not sure where to start, read on. I'm assuming you do not read Italian.

Let's start with the available Fiore resources. First and foremost, whether you read Italian or not, try to get a copy of Massimo Malipiero's *Il Fior di Battaglia*, as it includes a complete (if not terribly high resolution) reproduction of the Getty manuscript and some interesting historical material. It is regrettably out of print, but you can now download very high resolution copies of the manuscript from the internet. Coupled with Tom Leoni's translation, you have a readable version of the entire book. That's already vastly more to go on than I had back in 1994 when I began working on this art. The Pisani-Dossi manuscript is easily found online. Though there is not yet an authoritative translation, you can find complete and partial translations also online. As yet there are no generally available copies of the Morgan or the BnF versions, though copies may be had from their parent libraries.

We have only four secondary sources focused on Fiore: serious students will of course buy them all!

- *The Knightly Art of Battle*, by Dr. Ken Mondschein,
- *Fiore dei Liberi's Armizare, The Chivalric Martial Arts System of Il Fior di Battaglia*, by Robert N. Charrette.

And my own:

- *Mastering the Art of Arms vol.1: The Medieval Dagger*
- *The Armizare Vade Mecum*, mnemonic verses to help you remember the components of the Art.

It is also a good idea to read around your subject, and I highly recommend the following:

- *De Arte Gladiatoria*, by Filippo Vadi, was translated and published by Greg Mele and Luca Porzio in 2003 and again by me in 2012, as *Veni, VADI, Vici*. This is different from Fiore's work in several crucial ways, but shows signs of being part of the same tradition.
- *On Killing*, by Lt. Col. Dave Grossman, addresses the psychological aspects of violence, especially what it takes to be able to kill people.
- *Meditations on Violence* by Sgt. Rory Miller establishes the importance of the context that any given martial art is supposed to work in.

- *The Inner Game of Tennis* by W. Timothy Gallwey may seem out of place here, but is actually a fantastic source for getting to grips with the difficulties of learning new motor actions. This can cut your necessary training time to achieve competence in half.
- *The Art of Learning* by Josh Waitzkin. The title says it all, really.

The Sword

Your first sword should be blunt, for training with partners and against durable targets (such as hitting the tyre, for more on which, see p. 126). The blade should be of heat-treated spring steel, and it should measure between 110 and 130 centimetres (about 43 to 51 inches) from pommel to point. The weight should be absolutely no more than 1.8kg (just under 4 pounds) for even the longest sword in that range. For most people, a length of 120cm (47") and a weight of 1.6kg (3 1/2 pounds) is about right, with the balance point about 5cm (2 inches) from the crossguard. You ought to be able to fit three hands on the handle. Any shorter and it's not optimum for this style (we know this because Fiore has us at times grab our opponent's sword handle between his hands, so there must be space for three hands there!). Much longer and it starts to behave like a two-hander (and looks nothing like Fiore's illustrations).

My preferred suppliers for training longswords are Pavel Moc (www.swords.cz) in Europe, and Arms and Armor (www.armor.com) in America. My students in Asia and Australia tend to go for the European suppliers, which has more to do with shipping costs than anything else, I think.

Regarding the exact model or style, my best advice to anyone buying a sword is get the one you love. Spend a bit extra if you have to, because you will be spending hundreds and hundreds of hours with this weapon, and the more you love it the happier those hours will be. It's not worth economising by a few dollars if that means sacrificing the sense of "oh yes!" when you pick it up. I have often heard students trying out the swords we have for sale say something like "it's nice, but it's not *my* sword"—which is exactly as it should be. Somewhere inside you probably have a sense of what *your* sword is like, so get that one, or as close to it as you can find.

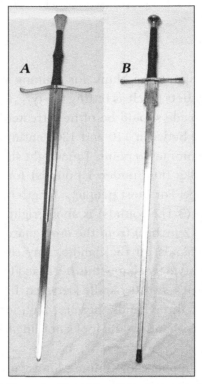

Training swords – **A** Durer by Pavel Moc; **B** Fechterspiele by Arms and Armor.

Clothing

When choosing the clothing you will train in, the primary choice is between accurate period clothing or modern gear. In a single night at work I might teach medieval sword and buckler, Fiore's Art, renaissance period rapier, and eighteenth century smallsword. I can't be changing clothes every five minutes to fit the next system, so at my school we all train in a t-shirt and track-suit trousers. If you are actively researching the Art, it is necessary to test all interpretations in accurately-made, period-correct clothing. (I have done so for you for everything in my books.) Period clothing can and does affect how you move, and what parts of your body are vulnerable. I would suggest that if your group is intending to focus on a single period, then it is worth investing in accurate period clothing. If you expect to train in styles from more than one period, then you will need to compromise (or get lots and lots of different sets of training clothes— I know many people for whom the clothing is half the fun).

Protective Gear

You wear protective gear for the convenience of your partner—it allows him to actually hit you in training. But do not for one second get the idea that your protective gear actually protects you from serious injury or death should your partner be a fool or a villain. This Art is intended for killing people who may be wearing a full suit of armour. Period technique is designed to kill people wearing period protection, so there must be a change either to the protective gear, or to the technique, if you wish to train without injury. I choose always to change the gear, not the action. We are trying to simulate unarmoured longsword combat done wearing a gambeson or padded jacket, so we must protect the body against thrusts, and the head, hands, elbows and knees against all blows.

In class, my students normally wear just a t-shirt, trousers and a fencing mask. Some also wear gloves. For careful pair practice, that's all you need. But for advanced training, freeplay, and freeplay preparation, you will need more gear or your partner's actions are so constrained that you won't be put under enough pressure.

Head Protection

In my salle, **all pair practice requires face protection**. You only have one pair of eyes, so look after them. For slow drills, and careful freeplay between advanced practitioners, a standard FIE international grade fencing mask is fine. They are not too expensive, and are easy to get. For faster work, and a more vigorous style of freeplay, you need better protection than the mask will give you. The best products on the market at the time of going to press, both designed for this art, are:

- That Guy's Product's (http://www.thatguysproducts.com/) Heavy Weapons mask by Terry Tindall: this has a suspension system like a helmet, and thanks to a miscommunication between me and a senior student during class one evening, I know that they can take a full force longsword blow without caving in. But it is a mask, not a helmet, so do not expect it to perform like one. Unfortunately, Terry has retired, so these are not currently available, but there are other manufactuers looking into making them again.
- Windrose Armory's Fiore sparring helm (http://www.windrosearmoury.com/): a proper helmet, but mass- produced and priced accordingly. It is fitted with a mesh or perforated face protection. You will be receiving thrusts to the face that can and will slip through a normal slit visor, so this mesh is essential. This is certainly the best head protection for the money.

I have tested both, and found them much more effective than fencing masks.

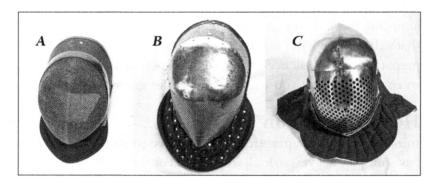

A Fencing mask; **B** Tindall mask; **C** Windrose helm

There used to be a pretty reliable way to identify a historical swords-manship enthusiast—plenty of scars, and fingers that wouldn't bend properly any more. After a broken finger and two cracked knuckles, I figured out two things: first, how to attack without exposing my hands, and second, that there is just no substitute for proper steel gauntlets. These can be clamshell (with broad overlapping plates covering all four fingers together, like mittens) or fingered (with individual sets of plates covering each finger). They must protect from above the wrist to the tips of your fingers, while allowing a full range of movement of the wrist, and a full range of movement of the sword. (Remember, we are not using these for armoured combat, but to simulate unarmoured combat safely.) The best solution is custom-made gadling gauntlets, where each phalange of the finger has its own steel shell, and each knuckle is protected by an exactly placed little dome. These run very expensive, and I find that a pair of mass-produced scale-fingered gauntlets (where the fingers are protected by overlapping scales) are fine. I personally don't like clamshell gaunt-lets, as they tend to restrict adjustments of your grip, but they are actually the best protection, and also the cheapest solution.

Scale gauntlets by Jiri Krondak

Incidentally, in my salle there are no substitutes permitted for steel gauntlets. Other options such as lacrosse gloves, ice-hockey gloves and similar sporting gloves are not an acceptable substitute for proper gauntlets, as they are just not designed to protect fingers from a steel sword. The modern plastic gauntlets made for longsword tournaments are not good either, in my experience, as they prevent you holding the sword properly, and I know too many people who have had bones broken wearing them. If you are waiting to save the money for gauntlets, there is a ton of material to practise that doesn't require them.

Body Armour

Our modern kit comprises:

- A fencing jacket, rated at least 500N (a standard measurement of resistance to penetration). For a more period feel, we use the Zen Warrior Armory fencing tunic (http:// www.zenwarriorarmory.com).
- A thick leather plastron, with collarbone and shoulder protection. These we get custom made.
- A gorget to protect the throat, with a lip to prevent sword points sliding over it
- Skating pads for elbows and knees
- A cup for men, and plastic breast protectors for women.

At the time of writing more and more of my students are opting for the new designed-for-longsword padded jackets from SPES Historical Fencing Gear, which seem to offer adequate protection and obviate the need for a separate plastron.

For period gear we have a much broader range of options, and any medieval clothing enthusiast probably knows more about the subject than I do. The gambeson, padded jack, aketon, arming jacket etc. all have much to offer, but make sure that the article you choose fits well, allows full freedom of movement of the arms, and adequately protects both collarbones and elbows. If you are going for the full period effect, you will run into trouble at the eyes and knees, so you may have to compromise a little on period accuracy.

Joni in full freeplay gear

Footwear

For period use, you have a range of flat, leather-soled boots and shoes to choose from. It is a very good idea for all students to train at least some of the time in period footwear on period surfaces (such as grass), as it has a greater effect on movement than any other item of dress. For modern training kit, I recommend flat, thin-soled training shoes. You absolutely do not want thick padding muffling the feel of the floor, especially when working on your structure. So running shoes and hiking boots are out! I often train alone barefoot, but insist on advanced drills and freeplay being done in shoes to protect the feet from being trodden on and hit by falling swords and other hazards. Also, small scraps of steel chipped off the swords can make nasty little splinters (one reason why my students mop the floor before every class).

Chapter Two

GENERAL PRINCIPLES

The Fundamental Theory of Martial Arts in General and Armizare in Particular

I n the later stages of this book you will come across a huge amount of instruction in the specifics of how to execute various techniques. When evaluating your execution of any given exercise it is useful to have a clear idea of the fundamental principles of the art. Solid theory is the single best feedback mechanism for students lacking an instructor. Not least so that if you are defeated in freeplay, or if a drill isn't working, you can figure out why and so fix the problem.

There are two sorts of knowledge: direct and derived (or, natural and contrived). A lake, a stone and a set-square illustrated this:

> The surface of a calm lake is level; it indicates the horizontal. A stone dropped into the lake falls straight down; it indicates the vertical. The stone hits the lake at a right angle.

> The set-square is an artificial device that has been created to consistently represent the same right angle that the lake and the stone embody without effort.

Describing the principles of the art of swordsmanship is exactly the same thing as creating a set- square to express the angle created by our (calm and peaceful) lake and our (beautifully faceted granite) stone. Well worth doing, of course, because when building something we can't be constantly dropping rocks into bodies of water. But the set-square will never be as accurate as the fundamental natural laws it is intended to embody.

It is also true that our lake is never perfectly level, as there are all sorts of factors like wind and fish swimming about disrupting its ideal flatness. Likewise, the rock is also affected by wind and by any slight impulse given it by your hand. So, in practice, the artificial set-square is generally more reliable, as these factors have been eliminated. It cannot be perfectly square, as even slight changes in temperature will affect the exact sizes of its component parts, but it will serve.

This rather long and whimsical analogy models the relationship between our actual experience of combat, and the general principles that govern combat itself. No one ever throws a perfect blow in the exact line it is supposed to be in—but by having a set of lines with which to classify blows, we can improve our own efforts, and respond more effectively to our opponent's. Fencing principles help us draw general conclusions from a basically chaotic situation. They impose a sense of order on it, to create a predictable result: our victory in combat.

Fiore's system is an intellectual construct overlaying and classifying a vast and unpredictable miscellany of possible actions. All such systems begin with experience—finding out what works and what doesn't. From those experiences, we extrapolate: if this worked here, will it work there? Once we have a batch of actions that seem to work, we look for patterns between them, and derive from those patterns common principles. This is not just how martial arts develop—it's how the human mind deals with the vast complexity of normal experience. After a while, principles harden into dogma, and may then be followed blindly and misapplied, leading to all sorts of problems. If we remember that in combat there is no time to think, and so our principles are effectively rationalizations made after the fact, we might use them more wisely.

With that in mind, what follows is my attempt to express the basic principles that underlie swordsmanship, and indeed many other martial arts.

Time, Measure, Structure, Flow

The fundamental aspects that define any given action are:

- Time
- Measure
- Structure
- Flow

Time

Every action has a beginning and an end—we measure the action by the time it takes to get from one to the other. Any counter to the action must occur at the correct point along that timeline. For example, my opponent tries to hit me on the head. I want to knock his blow aside and hit him. If I parry before he strikes, my action fails. If I try to parry after he strikes, he's already hit me. If I parry during his strike, it may work. We can in theory divide his strike into an infinite number of tiny units of time, but in practice, we can act against his blow at the following times:

1. Before it starts—we can prevent it ever happening
2. As he leaves his starting point
3. As he is about half way to the target
4. Just before he reaches the target
5. As he passes the target (this requires us to have avoided the blow).

The third or fourth time is the correct time to parry; the second to start a counterattack, the first in which to attack, anywhere between the second and fourth to avoid, and the fourth or fifth to strike after a parry (depending on whether the blow was parried at point 3 or 4).

Fiore's art makes most use of point three, with a firm parry after the attack is committed, but long before it lands.

Time also refers to the initiation of an action: which bit moves first? George Silver was, as far as I know, the first to write definitively on this subject, and in his 1599 *Paradoxes of Defence*, explains the following true (i.e. correct) timings:

- The time of the hand
- The time of the hand and body
- The time of the hand, body and foot
- The time of the hand, body and feet.

What this means is that the hand (i.e. the sword) moves first. Depending on your measure, you may also need to move your body and/or feet; if so, the movement goes hand, then body, then feet.

The sword should move first. Specifically, the point of the sword should move first. I will go into this in detail in the chapters on striking, but an image from the German tradition, to be found in Ms. 3227a (aka *The Nuremburg Hausbuch*) sums it up nicely: strike as if you had a piece of string tied to the point of your sword, and it was pulled suddenly into the target. This means your sword travels in the shortest possible line, as direct and fast as can be.

Measure

All fencing actions have their proper measure: the distance at which they are supposed to work. Unfortunately, Fiore does not discuss measure at all, but in later Italian fencing theory (specifically that of the early 17th-century rapier masters), measure is determined as simply the distance between the point of your sword and your opponent's target area. This works wonderfully with a rapier which is normally held pointing forwards, but is less perfect when using a longsword, as the point may be to the side, or even behind you. The position of the sword determines the length of the strike itself: how far the sword point has to travel from where it is to where it is going. The position of your feet and weight relative to the target determine how far you need to step during that motion of the sword to strike.

With the longsword we take both the motion of the sword and the footwork into account when determining measure, but as a general rule, measure is described according to what the feet have to do to accomplish your goal. As you approach your opponent you are either:

- Out of measure: it will take more than one step to strike
- In wide measure you can hit with your longest attack using a single foot movement. With the longsword this is a passing step
- In close measure you can hit without stepping
- Grappling measure: if you can reach your opponent's arms or body with your hand, you can grapple.

At any given time, your opponent will also be in one or other of these measures. Depending on the angle of approach, your reach, and the lengths of your swords, one of you may well be in (for instance) wide measure while the other is out of measure.

The ideal position to be in is such that you can strike without stepping, while your opponent has to step to strike.

Various masters at different times in fencing history have defined these measures a little differently or more precisely, but for our purposes, it is enough to know when you and your opponent can strike without stepping, need a single step, or need more than one step.

When attacking with a passing step, you are in fact doing all the work of getting from wide measure to close measure, while your opponent is being given the opportunity of close measure for no work at all. That first pass is a very dangerous moment in the fight, not least because as you pass, you are standing on one foot, while your opponent has both feet on the ground. "I could fight you standing on one leg" is a brave boast, and leads us directly into a discussion of structure.

Structure and Grounding

Strength comes from creating passive structures with your skeleton that will effortlessly and naturally direct the forces acting against you into the ground through one or other of your feet. This is called grounding. When you strike with a sword or anything else, the target strikes back with equal and opposite force. That force has to go somewhere, and it may well injure you or mess up your actions, if it is not safely routed into the ground. Your structure is the means by which we accomplish grounding.

Good structure is the foundation upon which all martial skill is based, and is the fundamental skill behind great feats of apparently magical ability. In short, it is as simple as making sure that for whatever you want to do, every one of the 200+ bones in your body is in exactly the right place, and every one of your 600+ muscles has exactly the right degree of tension. This takes some practice, but it is easy to acquire major technical improvement with relatively little work by minimizing as far as possible the unnecessary tension that inhibits your movement. Exercises to help you achieve this are included later in this book.

No matter what your structure, it will be stable in some directions, unstable in others, with a specific pattern of strength and weakness. Martial skill comes from making sure that you move from a strong position that does not inhibit your movement, through a succession of equally supported positions into your final position, with no resistance from unnecessary tension, so the work being done by your muscles is all available for creating the movement. And this movement is directed into your opponent's structure in a way that fully exploits the pattern of strength and weakness in his position.

Let us take a simple example: stand with your feet apart, pointed in the same direction as you are facing. Have a friend gently press from the side against one shoulder. You should find it easy enough to direct that pressure into the ground through the opposite foot.

Then have him apply the same gentle pressure into the centre of your chest, directly across the line between your feet. As you have no leg in that direction, you will either fall, or be forced to take a step to support yourself. In other words, you have to change your structure to adapt to the pressure.

 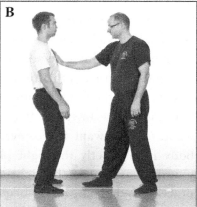

A Guy gently presses on Jukka's shoulder; he has no difficulty supporting it.
B Guy gently presses on Jukka's chest; he cannot support it.

Human beings are bipods—as any photographer could tell you, bipods are inherently unstable, which is why cameras are used with tripods. Imagine your opponent as a tripod—where would the third leg go? Any pressure in the direction of the imaginary third leg will be much more effective at destabilizing him than pressure directed into either one of his real legs. Likewise, as you move, you should be aware of your changing lines of strength and weakness. Naturally, it is ideal if your strikes are made in the line of your strength, directed into the line of your opponent's weakness.

I will reserve detailed discussion of the structural elements of the sword guards for the later practical chapters. At this point it is important that you grasp the idea that every position has an ideal structure, which is made up of lines of strength and weakness. You need be able to perceive and manipulate these lines. In general, where possible, apply your strength to his weakness. If his line is stronger, change your structure.

One of the hallmarks of good structure in a martial arts position is that it allows the techniques that are supposed to work from there to flow easily from it. I consider structure and flow as the fundamental elements of basic training.

Flow

Flow describes your freedom of movement at any time. Good technique should flow effortlessly from and through your perfectly structured guard positions. If your actions fail to flow, you should fix your structure. If your structure is wrong, you probably moved into it wrong: you failed to flow. Anything awkward or stuck *is wrong*. Things that flow well *might* be right.

In my experience, most students benefit from focusing on flow first, then structure.

You can destroy your opponent by breaking their structure, or by interrupting their flow. If you successfully maintain your structure and flow, you cannot fail. Nothing breaks structure and interrupts flow quite like a sword to the head!

So,

Flow creates structure, structure enables flow

Inside and Outside

There is a general convention in swordsmanship and many other martial arts to refer to actions being done "on the inside" or "on the outside". This refers to either the sword or the body—the front and the back of the swordsman.

As a right hander, if an opponent enters "on my inside", he will be on the left of my sword. If he enters on my outside, he will be on the right, and coming in over my sword arm. With the sword, assuming two right-handers, if the opponent's sword is on the left as I see it, we are both "inside". If his sword is on the right of mine, we are both "outside".

In general, operating on the outside leads you behind your opponent, but is structurally weaker; operating on the inside keeps you in front of him, but is structurally stronger.

The Sword: Divisions, Crossings and Binds

Swordsmanship treatises divide the blade into at least two parts: the strong (the part closest to the handle) and the weak (the part further away). Some go further, with four, six, eight or even twelve divisions. Fiore thankfully contents himself with three:

> *Tutta spada*: the "whole sword": the first third of the blade, nearest the hilt[4]
> *Mezza spada*: the middle third of the sword
> *Punta di spada*: the point or tip of the sword.

We need not be mathematically exact about these divisions: if contact is made near the tip, it's at the *punta*; if it's near the hilt, it's at the *tutta*; if it's near the middle, it's at the *mezza*. He describes these three divisions in the mounted combat section of the Morgan manuscript only, but all of the manuscripts explicitly divide the longsword techniques in sections according to where the crossing occurs.

In the Morgan, Fiore states that the *tutta* "withstands a little", the *mezza* "withstands less" and the *punta* "withstands nothing". This effectively describes what happens when the swords meet. The further away from the hand the point of contact, the less pressure you can withstand.

Unlike later systems, which use a sword that has more

---

4   Tom Leoni quite rightly points out (in his editorial correspondence) that Fiore (in the Morgan MS) uses the term "a tutta spada" adverbially, to describe a crossing done with the whole sword. It has become common usage in anglophone Fiore circles to use the term to describe what later sources would call the forte of the sword—the part of the blade near the hilt, at which the crossing in question is shown. I am less concerned with correct Italian usage than I am with convenient and current terminology, so have kept this barbarism over my esteemed colleague's objection.

comprehensive hand protection, we will almost invariably seek to parry with the middle of our sword against the middle of our opponent's. We will usually strike with one end of the sword (the punta) or the other (the pommel), though there are strikes done with just about every bit of the weapon.

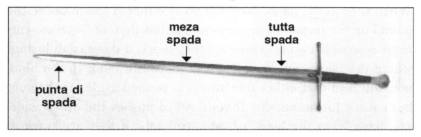

Fig: Divisions of the blade

Edge to Flat

Parries with the longsword are usually done as vigorous strikes to the attacking sword. Fiore often tells us to "beat the sword away". This should be done like any other strike: with the edge of your sword. Ideally, the parry should strike against the opponent's flat.

The sword is made such that it is stable in the plane of the edge, and unstable in the plane of the flat. Try bending a sword's blade and you'll see what I mean—the flats bend, the edges don't (if they do, buy a better sword!). Usually, your grip is such that you are also structurally supporting the edge. So you should ideally align your edge to your opponent's flat when parrying. This has the additional benefit, when working with sharp swords, of protecting your edge from damage by spreading the impact over a larger surface.

It is not always possible to find his flat though, so parries will sometimes meet edge to edge: better that than getting hit. Just don't try blocking with your flat. I once had a discussion about this with a friend who had picked up the idea that you should parry with your flat. I didn't have a sword on me at the time, and asked him to get a couple of his so we could try out his way versus mine. He told me all his swords were broken. I suggested that there might be a reason for that ...

The Bind

When the swords meet, they will do so either at the middles, the points or the *tutta*s, or some combination thereof, such as your *tutta* against his point. However they meet, if there is an instant where the blades are stuck, we say there is a bind. In the bind, you will find that either one sword is pushed aside, or they are both stuck in the middle. If your sword pushes the other aside, you have "won the bind" or "are stronger"; if they are stuck in the middle the bind is equal; if your sword has been pushed out of the centre, you have "lost the bind" or "are weaker". Almost every swordplay technique in Fiore's system flows from one or other of these binds.

In a perfect world, there is no bind: when you attack, your strike lands, smashing through any parry that might be attempted.When you defend, your parry beats aside the incoming sword and you can strike immediately. In the real world all sorts of things can go wrong, and it is of course possible to avoid the blades meeting altogether.

There are three critical variables to the bind, which are:

• Which parts of the blades are in contact (e.g. middle to middle, middle to point, point to *tutta* etc.)
• How close your opponent's blade is to you, and yours to him
• How much pressure is being exerted on the point of contact, and in what direction.

It is generally impossible to notice these consciously when actually fencing, but they do determine more than anything else what technique will be most effective after the crossing.

Wide and Close Play

Perhaps the most overt tactical distinction Fiore uses is between *zogho largo*, universally translated as "wide play", and *zogho stretto*, which may be translated as "close", "constrained" "narrow" or "tight" play. I find "constrained" to be the most accurate rendering, but "close" is currently the most common choice. This topic has produced perhaps the most persistent and widespread disagreement amongst Fiore scholars, so I will go into some detail regarding what I think these concepts mean, and how I use them.

Fiore's plays of the sword in two hands are clearly divided into the 20 plays of the *zogho largo* and the 23 plays of the *zogho stretto*. There are also plays done with the sword in one hand, in armour, and on horseback. The distinction between, say, the plays of the sword in armour and those of the sword on horseback are pretty obvious. The distinction between what constitutes *zogho largo* and what constitutes *zogho stretto* has been far less clear. In my first book, I defined the terms *gioco largo* (wide play) and *gioco stretto* (close play) as functions of measure: when you are close enough to touch your opponent with your hand, you are in *gioco stretto*. If you can reach him with your sword using one step or fewer, you are in *gioco largo*. This is a useful distinction to make, especially when classifying and cataloguing techniques.

For many years, this stood as the standard interpretation of *zogho largo* and *zogho stretto*, however, this is clearly not how Fiore uses the terms. (Remember our earlier discussion of changes in interpretations? Here you can see my pressure-test system in action.) In *il Fior di Battaglia*, we clearly see actions done close-in but placed in the *zogho largo* section (such as the 14th play of the second master), and actions done from quite far away placed in the *zogho stretto* (such as the 12th play). So what, then, do "wide" and "close" play refer to?

Simply put, the relationship between the two swords when they cross. There is a plethora of circumstances in which you are free to leave the crossing and strike as you will—these are all considered "*largo*". In other circumstances the conditions of the bind are such that if you leave the crossing you will immediately be struck. In these cases you are constrained to enter in under cover, and use one of the "close plays".

In practice, the type of crossing that demands close play is very specific: you must be crossed at the middle of the swords, with the points in presence (i.e. threatening the target) and sufficient pressure between the swords such that if one player releases the bind, he will be immediately struck. Ideally both players have their right foot forwards, which makes it easier to enter in. This is a situation of equality, in which either player should do the close play techniques.

In all other circumstances, most commonly when the opponent's sword has been beaten aside, it is safe to leave the crossing to strike your opponent. This is the fundamental condition of wide play. If it is necessary to maintain contact with the opponent's sword and enter to grapple or pommel strike, you are constrained to the close play. So, the plays are ordered according to the kind of crossing that they follow. These conditions exist in a continuum. As the opponent's sword gets closer, and the bind gets firmer, your ideal response changes. As it switches from "leave the bind and strike" (*largo*) to "keep in contact with the bind and enter" (*stretto*), so you will find your ideal response in one section of the book or the other. Identifying these conditions is perhaps the key tactical distinction to make in this system. Note that close play techniques can often be done in a wide play situation, but wide play techniques cannot be done from a close-play crossing without extreme risk. The techniques we see in the 10th, 14th, and 15th plays of the second master of the *zogho largo* (crossed at the middle of the swords) section are clearly "close", and there is no practical distinction between for example the 10th play here and the 2nd play of the *zogho stretto*. It's apparent then that we have a choice: either Fiore organised his book as a catalogue of techniques arranged by the measure in which they occur, with several errors, or ordered them according to the tactical circumstances in which they should be done, with no errors. Which would you choose?

As a rule of thumb, if your opponent's sword is moving towards you, or pressing in, you must bind it to prevent it from hitting you (*stretto*). If it is moving away from you, you can simply strike (*largo*).

Wide and close play describe *what happens*, but can also be used to describe a set of tactical preferences, an approach to the fight. When fencing an opponent who is much more comfortable in wide play, we may engineer a situation where only close play techniques will work. We can also of course deny a close-playing opponent the context he wants, and slip away into wide play as he tries to constrain us. A good fencer will be comfortable with both contexts, though most people have a preference for one type of play or the other. Please refer to the technical exercises later in the book for practical examples.

It is critically important that any set drill includes clear instructions for establishing a specific crossing, so that the technique being trained is done in its proper tactical context. Perhaps the most difficult thing when practising is to make sure that the crossing is correct—we naturally focus on the fun stuff, like hitting. So a lot of poor training occurs when the attack and parry meet in a way that would lead to one technique, but the set drill calls for another, and so the students end up practising (in good faith) the wrong response to the situation they are creating. So take your time and make sure that the crossings you are creating lead to the technique you are practising.

Principles from Fiore

Fiore explicitly discusses some principles of his art, in three main places:

1. The introduction, where he determines the eight things you need for success in *abrazare*

2. The beginning of the dagger section, where he determines the five things you need to know to defend yourself against a dagger attack

3. The segno page, which ends the sword out of armour section, and begins the sword in armour section, where he describes four virtues, *forteza, presteza, avvisamento,* and *ardimento.*

Let's discuss them in the order that they occur in the manuscript. **The eight things**[5] you need in *abrazare* (wrestling) are:

1. Strength
2. Speed
3. Knowledge of grips
4. Knowledge of how to break limbs
5. Knowledge of how to apply joint locks (*ligadure,* binds)
6. Knowledge of where to strike (the "places of pain"!)
7. Knowledge of how to throw your opponent to the ground
8. Knowledge of how to dislocate limbs.

Fiore states that *abrazare* is the foundation of his Art. So how should we apply these principles to swordsmanship? Of course, once we get into close quarters, longsword fighting has much in common with wrestling, and at that range we can take the principles exactly as read. While further away, how about this:

1. Strength (self-explanatory)
2. Speed (likewise)
3. Knowledge of grips—how to hold the sword properly
4. Knowledge of how to break an opponent's attack—beating it aside
5. Knowledge of how to bind his sword

---

5   As an interesting aside, the Pisani-Dossi manuscript lists seven things, in far less detail: strength, speed of hand and foot, advantageous grips, breaks, locks, strikes and wounds (*lesion*).

6. Knowledge of where to strike—especially important if he is wearing armour
7. Knowledge of how to get your opponent off-balance
8. Knowledge of how to disarm him (dislocating the sword from his grip).

This does not match up perfectly, and I have no idea whether Fiore intended these to be used this way, but it seems to work in practice.

The five things you need to know how to do when defending against the dagger are:

1. To take your opponent's dagger
2. To strike
3. To break their arms
4. To lock and counterlock
5. To throw him/her to the ground.

Notice that with the exception of the taking of the dagger, these are the same as we needed in *abrazare*: there is only one "addition", which, if we allow the dislocations to stand for the disarm (taking the dagger), is implied in the first group anyway. The three not mentioned are strength, speed and knowledge of grips. I am assuming that as strength and speed are clearly universal qualities, so knowledge of grips may be considered one too.

The Four Virtues

In the segno page, Fiore illustrates the four virtues a swordsman must possess. They are:

Forteza: strength. This is represented by an elephant with a tower on its back. Strength is not simply muscle power, but, as the image suggests, requires correct structure.

Presteza: speed. This is represented by a tiger holding an arrow, but is not merely speed of execution. I think of this as flow, evoked through the images of the arrow in the sky representing lightning, and the swift flow of the tiger's namesake, the River Tigris.

Avvisamento: foresight. This is represented by a lynx holding dividers; symbols of good eyesight and accurate measurement. This refers to judgment of time and measure.

Ardimento: boldness, courage. This is represented by a lion holding a heart, a symbol of lion- hearted valour.

The Pisani-Dossi manuscript uses the same symbols, and latin terms for the same virtues: *fortitudo, celeritas, audatia* and *prudentia.*

Mysteries

There remain several points of theory to which Fiore refers but he does not provide enough information to create an authoritative interpretation. Some readers will be surprised by the omissions later if I don't cover them now, so here are the two most commonly asked about:

The turns of the sword: after defining three footwork turns: stable, half and full (which I will address in detail in Chapter Three: Footwork p. 52–72) Fiore goes on to say that there are also three turns of the sword. What a stable turn of the sword is, or a half turn, or a full turn, we have no way of knowing for certain; there is just no internal evidence to go on. I have my theories, but they are only theories. As he never tells us to perform any one of them, it takes nothing away from the execution of the plays to simply leave that distinction out.

The stable and unstable guards: in the Getty manuscript only, the illustrations of the twelve guards of the sword are all titled in red, and after the name of the guard there is a single word, *stabile, instabile* or *pulsativa*. Lots of theories have been floated as to what exactly these mean, but there is no evidence in the text to support any one of them. For example, the text for *posta breve*, a *stabile* guard, begins: "this is *posta breve*, that wants a long sword. It is a malicious guard that does not have stability."

(My translation.) So this "stable" guard doesn't have "stability". Nowhere in the text does Fiore explain what these terms mean, nor does he use them anywhere other than the titles for the guards. So they cannot be definitively interpreted from internal evidence, and nor are they necessary to use the guards effectively according to the explanations that he does give us. So again I have left these terms out.

There is plenty of material to work with without chasing after unanswerable questions or resorting to conjecture. I will reserve judgment on these terms until further evidence comes to light— perhaps another copy of the book will be found that will solve these puzzles.

Mindset

Imagine a gunnery captain with a team of four cannon, each cannon manned by four men. The captain's job is to make sure the cannon are pointed in the right direction, and go off at the right time. The men do the rest (loading, firing, swabbing out, etc.). A well-trained and efficient team smashes the enemy fortifications into dust. Contrast this with the situation should the gunnery captain insist on loading, aiming and firing every cannon himself, personally, "no, put that cannonball down, I'll load this baby ..."

This analogy aptly models the relationship between your conscious, decision-making mind and the part of your brain that actually tells which muscles to contract and when, to move you around. A huge part of effective training is simply getting the gunnery captain to stop interfering with his highly competent team, and get on with his job while they get on with theirs. In other words, get out of the way and let good technique happen. Good technique is always mechanically efficient, and so is quickly picked up by the part of your brain that has been learning new tricks since before you mastered walking.

To work on a movement you need:

- A clear picture or feeling of how it is now
- A clear picture or feeling of how it should be
- A real-time feedback mechanism for identifying the difference.

And that's it. Your worker mind will do the rest. Just pay attention with your watching mind, and notice, without attachment or expectation, what is happening—how the action is changing towards the preferred mode of execution.

You may find that your busy, intrusive, self-absorbed watcher is hard to quiet down. I don't bother trying—I prefer distraction. Give yourself something useful and interesting to focus on, such as a specific aspect of what you are doing, and let yourself *pay attention* but not *interfere*.

One of the more difficult aspects of historical swordsmanship is that ideals change. As the research develops our idea of how things should be done, so we have to change our physical practice. My students often complain about having to change the habits that they have diligently built up. It took me years, and reading *The Inner Game of Tennis*, before I realized how it is that as my interpretation changes, my actions seem to automatically change to the new way of things. I never work to "change a habit". Once the new interpretation is made, I don't fall back into the "old" way. The trick is startlingly simple:

Don't change old habits. Create new ones. See the new action clearly in your head, and then allow yourself to do it. Think of it as entirely new and distinct from any previous way of doing things, so you never find yourself trying to correct a motion in mid-flow.

And Finally

A good swordsman, or indeed a good martial artist, from any style or culture, can be identified by a certain something; grace, speed, effortless power, modesty, a bit of flash and dash—we really don't have a word for it in English. The Italians, however, do:

Sprezzatura

Literally "studied negligence", nonchalance (again, not really an English word!). In fencing, *sprezzatura* can only be accomplished if clean, accurate technique flows effortlessly out of your perfect, graceful structure, putting you in exactly the right place at the right time to effortlessly overcome your opponent in an aesthetically pleasing way. Aim for this.

Chapter Three

FOOTWORK: STEPPING AND TURNING

Footwork is getting to the right place at the right time. "Good" footwork allows you to control measure, and hence control timing. It also ensures that once you have established good structure, you can maintain it while in the flow.

In short: **footwork is how you get to the right place at the right time to strike safely.**

In medieval sources it is very rare for footwork to be clearly defined or described, so perhaps the single most important passage in *Il Fior di Battaglia* comes on p. 22 recto. This is the only description of footwork that Fiore gives us, in the paragraph that begins the section of the longsword held in two hands. It is worth translating the text here in full, as it defines the terms upon which any practical interpretation must be based. It is also the only time in which Fiore actually explains any of the terms he uses. This text sits above an illustration of two swordsmen holding their weapons on their right shoulders (my translation).

We are two guards, one made like the other, and one is the counter to the other. And with each of the other guards in the art, one similar to the other is the counter, except for the guards that stand with the point in line: thus 'posta longa' (long position), and 'breve' (short) and 'mezza porta di ferro' (middle iron gate), because point against point, the longer strikes first. And what one guard can do the other can do. And each guard can do 'volta stabile' (stable turn) and 'mezza volta' (half turn). 'Volta stabile' is when standing firm, one can play in front and behind on one side. 'Mezza volta' is when one makes a pass forwards or backwards, and so can play on the other side in front or behind. 'Tutta volta' (whole turn) is when you turn one foot around the other foot: one foot stays firm, and the other circles around it. And therefore I say the sword has three movements, thus: 'volta stabile', 'mezza volta' and 'tutta volta'. These guards are called one and the other (i.e. both) 'posta di donna' (woman's position). Also there are four things in the art, thus: 'passare' (pass), 'tornare'(return), 'acressere' (increase, i.e. step forward) and 'discressere' (decrease, i.e. step backwards).

A Jan in *posta di donna*, forward weighted;
B Jan in *posta di donna*, rear weighted.

When I began studying Fiore's work in 1994, I started with the Pisani-Dossi manuscript, which doesn't discuss footwork at all. I saw from the pictures that the swordsman's weight is sometimes forwards, on the front leg, and sometimes to the rear, and that the action was not precisely linear: the feet turn. So I worked out "the shift between forward position and rear position", and only years later learned (from Bob Charron in 2003, who was working from the Getty MS) that this is the *volta stabile*.

You can see it from the two versions of *posta di donna* shown here: in each case the sword is on the right shoulder, so the only change is in the legs (the feet have not left the ground, hence the "stable turn").

Note that in the illustration the point of view has also moved, from the right to the left side. The pass is also clearly visible in many plays throughout the book, and needs no real discussion. Likewise, *tornare*, to pass backwards, is stated and shown in several places.

Let's begin with something simple: standing. Creating a decently structured guard position first requires that you have a sense of what good structure does, so let's build that from the ground up.

Where should your weight be on your feet?

Standing Drill

You will need a partner, and some patience.

1. Begin with your feet parallel.
2. Rock your weight back onto your heels.
3. Have your partner apply gentle pressure with a single finger in the middle of your chest. Do not resist it, but try to direct the pressure down into your feet. See how much pressure is needed before you are obliged to step to maintain your balance.
4. Repeat the drill, with your weight a little closer to your toes. Is that more stable, or less?
5. Keep changing the point on the soles of your feet where your weight rests, until you find and go past the best, most stable point.

You should find that the position gets more and more stable up to a point, and then starts getting weaker again. Find that best place again, and remember it.

Guy helping Jukka with the standing drill

Now let's repeat the process with your tailbone. Start with it sticking out behind you like a tail, and gradually, testing each change, bring it up and under your pelvis until it is pointing forwards.

Somewhere between the two extremes is the ideal structure for your lower spine. It is important to roll the tailbone like closing a fist; do not push it forwards.

At some point, you will almost certainly have started bending your knees, sinking your weight onto your feet to become more stable. Most of the time, such as when sitting, standing or walking, the primary force acting on your position is gravity, which is working vertically, straight down. For martial arts purposes, we also need to be able to deal with forces acting horizontally, usually coming at us from the front. The ideal structures for resisting these two very different forces are obviously different, so by all means play with the positions as you are sitting, standing, and walking, and all the time try to find the structure that allows you to absorb and direct the forces in play with the minimum muscular effort.

Once you can reliably create something close to the correct (because more stable) structure for standing and dealing with forces coming from in front of you, it's time to take a look at the basic stance. This does not change, though it has a forward weighted and a back weighted form.

Juhani stands on guard forwards weighted

Note the following key points:

- Your weight is primarily on one foot
- Your back is relaxed, straight, balanced easily over your pelvis
- Your back leg is relaxed, extended but with the knee soft
- Your weight falls on the ball of the weighted foot.

See if you can find this stance by establishing a good standing structure, then shifting your weight onto one foot, then stepping out, forwards or backwards, to create the guard.

Regarding the position of the back heel, some illustrations show it clearly raised, while others seem to show it flat. In my opinion, the key difference is the position of the hips. If the hips are turned forwards, the back heel is dragged up. If the rear hip is turned back (so the pelvis is in line with the front foot), then the back heel falls. The most common variant is to keep the hips about 45°

from the line between your feet, a comfortable compromise. If this is unfamiliar territory for you, try it as a drill:

- Stand with your left foot forwards and:
- Weight on the front foot
- Hips turned clockwise, so your pelvis is lined up with the line between your feet (as far as your current flexibility allows)
- Back (right) foot flat on the ground
- From this position, turn your hips gradually anti-clockwise until your pelvis is at right angles to the line between your feet
- It ought to be necessary for your back (right) heel to rise off the ground to allow your right hip to travel so far forwards
- Try this again on the other side.

A Ville stands on guard with his hips in line (here to maximise the reach of his right hand); **B** Ville stands on guard with his hips across the line (here because his left hand is also reaching forwards)

This directly affects the lines of strength and weakness of the position. Your front foot is pointing directly forwards. For maximum stability in the line of the foot, your pelvis should be parallel with that line. For maximum stability across the line of the foot, your pelvis should be at right angles to it.

The Four Steps

When walking normally, one foot passes the other. This is the basis of longsword footwork.

The pass forwards (*passo*) is simply a matter of passing your back foot forwards, re-establishing your stance with the other leg forwards.

Passare: Juhani passes forwards with his left foot

The pass back (*tornare*) is the same thing in reverse: move your front foot behind you and re-establish your stance.

Tornare: Juhani passes back with his left foot

It is also useful to be able to advance and retire without passing, to adjust measure or generate force. These are the *accrescere* and *discressere*.[6]

Accrescere: Juhani steps forwards with is front (right) foot, and brings up his back (left) foot to re-establish the same position.

Starting in your stance, push your weight forwards, allowing the front foot to move to support it. *There is no need to pull your weight off the front foot before you move it.* Finish by bringing up your back foot the same distance, so your stance is restored.

Discrescere: Juhani steps back with his back (left) foot, then his front foot to re-establish the position.

---

6   *Accrescere*: The treatise includes many statements along the lines of "I advance the foot that is in front a little out of the way and with the left I pass diagonally", or more colloquially "I step my front foot off the line and pass across". It is clearly an action that moves one foot, that is neither a pass nor a turn. The term literally means "to increase", and it is generally accepted that it is a movement of one foot, without passing, in the general direction of the opponent (i.e. forwards). The discressere ("to decrease") is by inference a step back without passing.

Starting in your stance, push your weight backwards, allowing your back foot to move to support it. Adjust your front foot back to restore your stance. With both the *accrescere* and *discrescere*, the step should be done with a single motion of your weight in the desired direction.

This takes some practice, and some faith that when you shift your weighted foot you're not going to fall over. Every unnecessary motion is an opportunity for your opponent to hit you.

The Three Turns:

To get a handle on the difference between passing, as above, and turning, get up and walk normally across the room. Notice the way your hands move. Your left hand goes forward with your right foot; your right hand goes with your left foot. This keeps your lower back, hips, and shoulders, stable as you move. Now deliberately co-ordinate your right hand and right foot and walk across the room like that. You will find that your whole body naturally turns with every step. You probably find it feels strange and awkward. Sword in hand, you will usually unite the right foot and right hand, left foot and left hand, as the turning of the hips helps generate power. Fiore defines these turns by the way the feet move. If they stay in place, you're doing a stable turn (*volta stabile*). If you pass forwards or backwards, it's a half turn (*meza volta*). If you pivot on one foot while the other turns around it, it's a whole turn (*tutta volta*). Let's take them one at a time.

When executing the *volta stabile*, it is essential that you unify your forces such that every part of the body is moving in the same direction. The turn is about 135°, and it often helps to use the unarmed *posta longa* or *posta frontale* to establish direction, as illustrated.

Volta stabile: Juhani starts right foot forwards with his weight
on his front leg. He pivots to his left on the balls of his feet
about 135° and finishes with his weight on his left leg.

The *mezza volta*, on one level, is just a pass (a step where one foot passes the other) backwards or forwards. It is stated in the text that you can play on the other side, so it is reasonable to infer that it may be accompanied by a turn of the hips. I interpret the addition "in front and behind" to refer to the direction of the pass.

The *tutta volta* is wide open to interpretation. Strictly speaking, any time one foot turns around the other, in any direction or any distance, it's a *tutta volta*. In practice, it is used as either an adjusting step to align yourself with the *strada,* which is the direct line between you and your opponent:

Juhani shifts the orientation of his stance a few degrees by pivoting
on his front (left) foot and bringing his back (right) foot around.

Or it's used to generate force in a turn, when performing a close play technique.

Juhani starts left foot forwards and sweeps
his back leg around to turn a full 180°.

It's a good idea to practise these turns on their own and in sequence, until you are familiar with the actions and the terminology.

Exploiting Your Strength and Your Opponent's Weakness

As we discussed in the chapter *General Principles*, because human beings are bipods, any pressure in the direction of the imaginary third leg will be much more effective at destabilising them than pressure directed into either one of their real legs. Likewise, as you move, you should be aware of your lines of strength and weakness. Ideally, your strikes are directed in the line of your strength and into the line of your opponent's weakness. This is why most defensive footwork is diagonal: you place your line of stability along your opponent's line of weakness.

Finding lines of weakness: **A** Auri has stepped in with an attack: **B** Guy has stepped to her inside, along her line of weakness; **C** Guy steps behind her along the same line.

This is why Fiore's most frequently repeated footwork instruction is the step offline followed by a pass across. I do this sequence as one smooth diagonal movement of the weight.[7] If the left foot is forwards, you will go diagonally forwards to the left.

---

7   Fiore describes this action as: "*subito acresse lo tuo pe che denanci fora de strada u cum laltro pe passa ala traversa anchora fora de strada*": "Immediately step your front foot off the line, and with the other foot pass across, also off the line" (This example from the *scambiar di punta*, f26v). The *accrescimento fora di strada* is simple enough: step your front foot off the line (left for the left foot or right for the right foot: do NOT cross your feet!). *Passo ala traversa* is a bit more tricky, though reference to the accompanying illustrations suggests that the equivalent English expression "pass on the traverse", or simply "traverse", common in English fencing manuals, would serve as a translation. (Note though that some manuals use the term to describe a sideways or diagonal step without passing, e.g. Roworth, pp. 41–43.) Putting this all together, it seems that to pass *ala traversa* is to pass diagonally forwards or to the side (i.e. on the traverse, and specifically not straight forwards). As I see it, it is passing the back foot across the strada—hence 'pass across'.

1. Stand on guard, left foot forwards
2. Keeping your weight forwards, shift your left foot about eight inches off the line to the left
3. And pass diagonally left: the direction is about 30° to the left of straight ahead
4. Repeat with the right foot forwards.

A Ken starts on guard with his left foot forward; **B** and steps his left foot off the line to the left, **C** and passes across

At my school we have a standard drill, in three parts, for working on this sequence. When practising this drill, it is crucial to note the following:

- Each combination (step and three passes or turns) must be done as one smooth movement of the weight
- Use the *accrescere* to kickstart the movement of your weight
- Your weight only moves in the one, diagonal, direction.

This is one of those drills that looks extremely tricky and complicated on the page, but is relatively simple in action.

- Stand on guard, left foot forwards
- *Accrescere fora di strada* (step the front foot off the line)
- *Passo ala traversa* (pass across)

- Pass again in the same direction, on the same line
- Pass again in the same direction, on the same line.

You are now right foot forwards. Make an adjustment so you are facing in the original direction (this makes it easier to orient yourself with the room). Repeat on the right side. You are now left foot forwards again. Readjust to orient yourself, then:

1. *Accrescere fora di strada* (step the front foot off the line)
2. *Tutta volta*, passing the right foot behind you, turning on the ball of the left foot until you are facing in the same diagonal as before pass again in the same direction, on the same line pass again in the same direction, on the same line.

We see that the *tutta volta* can take us to exactly the same place as a pass. We can then repeat the same thing starting with the right foot forwards, then:

1. *Accrescere fora di strada* (step the front foot off the line)
2. *Passo ala traversa* (pass across). The direction is about 30° to the left of straight ahead
3. *Tutta volta*, passing the right foot behind you, turning on the ball of the left foot until you are facing in the same diagonal as before
4. Pass again in the same direction, on the same line. The second pass has been replaced with a *tutta volta*. Repeat on the other side, then
5. *Accrescere fora di strada* (step the front foot off the line)
6. *Passo ala traversa* (pass across). The direction is about 30° to the left of straight ahead
7. Pass again in the same direction, on the same line
8. *Tutta volta*, passing the right foot behind you, turning on the ball of the left foot until you are facing in the same diagonal as before.

And repeat on the other side.

So, this exercise replaces each of the three passes in order, with a *tutta volta*. You can find examples of these sequences in use in sword techniques later in this book.

Pass Out of the Way

Depending on the precise circumstances (which will be explored in depth later), defensive footwork is usually executed on a line diagonal to that of the attack. We have seen how to get there in the direction of the front foot (when the left foot is forwards, go left; when the right foot is forwards, go right). But what about when you are left foot forwards and need to go to the right?

This is where the *passo fora di strada* comes in: pass out of the way. This step is often accompanied by a shift of the other foot behind you, to align yourself better with the opponent's line of weakness.[8]

A Ilpo starts on guard, left foot forwards **B** and passes out of the way with his right foot, **C** completing the step by bringing his left foot around.

1. Stand on guard, left foot forwards
2. Pass diagonally forwards and to the right with your right foot
3. Bring your left foot around behind you, so you now face diagonally left

---

8 In *The Swordsman's Companion* I described this sequence as the 135/90 step, or the ideal step.

4. Reset, right foot forwards and repeat, stepping left with your left foot.

You can think of this step as a turning action (it is in fact a *mezza volta*); you want to get to a position where you are facing diagonally left, while having moved over to the right.

Four Guards

Fiore begins his treatise with four guards:

- *Posta longa*: long position, both arms extended, but one forwards and one back (think: grab his throat)

Jan in *posta longa*.

- *Posta di dente di zenghiaro*: the guard of the wild boar's tusk: arms are bent at the elbow, with the forward hand thrusting up (think: break his jaw)

Jan in *dente di zenghiaro*.

- *Posta di porta di ferro*: the guard of the iron door, both hands down (think: throw his head on the ground)

Jan in *posta di tutta porta di ferro*.

- *Posta frontale*: frontal position, both hands up and forwards (think: thumbs in eyes).

Jan in *posta frontale*.

For our purposes, these guards are most usefully thought of as the fundamental way-points of every movement. If I wish to stab you in the face with my dagger, which is on my belt, and both my hands are down, I go from hands down (*porta di ferro*), draw my dagger up (*dente di zenghiaro*), and stab you, extending the arm (*posta longa*).

You might defend yourself by attacking me while I'm still in *porta di ferro*; entering as my hand rises into *zenghiaro*, or by intercepting my hand as it goes towards *longa*. Any later, and of course you are hit, unless you get out of the way.

A Julia stands with the dagger down, **B** lifts it to strike and **C** strikes.

This applies equally to all weapons. A sword strike, from the right shoulder, into and through a target, is created by moving through these same basic positions. If we remove the weapon, the start position is analogous to *zenghiaro*: the arm is bent. As the strike lands, the arm is going to *longa* or *frontale*, and it arrives in *porta di ferro*. With the sword in hand, some of these guards have different names, but the principle remains. By learning to move through these positions, you create the base upon which you can add any weapon you like.

In my salle, most basic Fiore classes begin with "the Four Guards Drill", which has you combine the four guards with the three turns. It is a specific reference to our main source, a familiar starting point (once you know it), and a way to get into the proper way of moving without distraction. It goes like this:

1. Start in *posta longa*, right hand and foot forwards (because this is how it is shown in the treatise)
2. Establish the line you will walk along—if you are indoors, make it parallel to one wall
3. Leading with your left hand, *volta stabile* into *longa* on the left
4. Leading with your right hand, *volta stabile* back to where you started

5. Leading with the left hand, *mezza volta* to *posta longa* on the left, along the *strada*
6. Leading with the right hand, *volta stabile* into *zenghiaro*
7. Leading with the left hand, *volta stabile* into *zenghiaro*
8. Leading with the right hand, *mezza volta* into *zenghiaro*
9. Leading with both hands, *volta stabile* into *frontale*
10. Leading with both hands, *volta stabile* into *porta di ferro*
11. Leading with both hands, *mezza volta* into *frontale*
12. Leading with both hands, *volta stabile* into *porta di ferro*
13. You can now *volta stabile* into *longa* on the left side, and repeat everything the other way around.

When you run out of space, in either direction, use a *tutta volta* to turn yourself around, elegantly and in style, into the next guard of the sequence and continue.

At this point, the pattern should be clear: your feet go *volta stabile, volta stabile, mezza volta, volta stabile, volta stabile, mezza volta;* while your hands go *longa, longa, longa, zenghiaro, zenghiaro, zenghiaro, frontale, porta di ferro, frontale, porta di ferro.*

We use this exercise mostly as a segue from the normal modern world we live in, into the special environment of the school, and as a specific reference to our primary source. I'm sure by the time you've worked through this book you will have a dozen ways to adapt, alter, and customise this exercise to suit your own needs and interests.

Opposite page: **A** Ilpo begins in right side posta longa; **B** and volta stabiles to longa on the left; **C** and volta stabiles back to longa on the right; **D** and passes into longa on the left; **E** and volta stabiles into zenghiaro on the right; **F** and volta stabiles to zenghiaro on the left; **G** and passes to zenghiaro on the right; **H** and volta stabiles to frontale, left foot forwards; **I** and volta stabiles to porta di ferro, right foot forwards; **J** and passes to frontale, left foot forwards; and **K** volta stabiles to porta di ferro, right foot forwards. The next action would be a volta stabile into longa on the left, and repeating the entire drill from there.

Moving Freely

Once the static forms of the footwork are comfortable, it is a good idea to develop your ability to apply it unconsciously. In practice, I introduce this kind of playful exercise before most students have mastered the static forms, then point out that the steps they just did naturally were the same as the ones they were learning as a static drill. Feel free to do likewise. For this we have several exercises, my favourite of which is the stick game. Played in pairs, it looks like this:

- One player (A) has a stick, the other (B) doesn't. B stands on guard
- A gently swings the stick at him
- B steps as necessary to avoid the stick and get behind A, tapping him on the back
- A moves away, and strikes again.

You can also add penalties for getting hit, such as three push-ups.

Played in class, one student or the teacher has the stick, and charges about trying to tap people, who have to get out of the way and touch his back. This works best if everyone is obliged (on pain of push-ups) to keep moving (we usually start with everyone practising the step and three passes drill before bringing out the stick), and the person wielding the stick is careful to only hit people who are making mistakes, like flinching or losing their guard positions. With a bit of practice, this is a good workout for everyone, and teaches the most important lesson of footwork:

> Footwork is how you get to the right place
> at the right time to strike safely.

Chapter Four

ONE STRIKE, ONE DEFENCE

This chapter contains the nucleus of all swordsmanship training, and as such should provide you with the foundation on which you will build the rest of your art. Let's start with picking up the weapon.

Holding the Sword

The purpose of the grip is to form a seamless interface between you and the weapon, allowing you to manipulate the sword as necessary. The sword is a tool, a labour-saving device. Most of the time, we will want to be hitting things with the edge or the point, so our grip must allow us to deliver force through those parts of the blade. Pick a target: a bit of wood screwed to the wall will do, anything that doesn't mind a few dents. Then pick up your sword with one hand and poke the target, gently. Don't think about it, just do it. Now press down on the floor with the edge, hard enough that it's difficult to stop the blade bending sideways. Imagine that you are trying to crush a tomato. Still one-handed, write your name in the air with the point, as beautifully as you can and as large as you like. Chances are, you are now holding the sword correctly.

Now, what do we do with the left hand? Usually, grip the pommel to support our efforts with the edge. Try all of the above exercises using your left hand to help your right.

Now that we have the sword in hand, we need to notice that one edge faces away from us, and is easy to hit things with: that's the true edge (*filo dritto*). The other faces towards us: that's the false edge (*filo falso*).

Just to make sure we're on the same page, here are some

pictures of my hand on the sword. Notice that the sword is either held back against the web of the thumb, with the blade close to 90° to the forearm, or point forwards almost in line with the forearm, and the hilt resting in the heel of the hand. The shift between these two positions is a key part of most blows and parries. When the sword is held back, the grip is "chambered" (like a bullet in a gun, ready to strike); when the sword is extended, it is "released". In most circumstances, when the sword is held close to the body, away from the opponent, the grip should be chambered, and when the sword strikes or parries, it should be released. I will deal with specific exceptions as they arise.

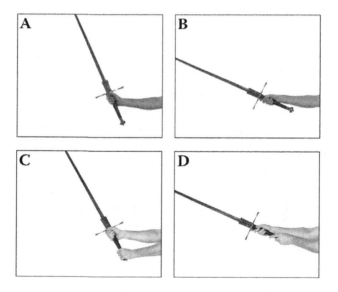

A grip one hand point back; B grip one hand point forward;
C grip two hands, point back; D grip two hands, point forwards.

Teaching the proper grip is tricky, as adjustments that are invisible to the naked eye can have major consequences in using the weapon. As a general rule, align the part of the grip that corresponds to the false edge with the lifeline of your palm, and shake hands with the sword. Keep your grip as relaxed as possible to allow the sword freedom of movement. The weight of the sword rests on the middle phalange of the middle finger, and the back of the handle presses into the middle of the heel of the hand. You should be able to hold the sword with just those points of contact; try taking off your forefinger, ring finger, little finger and thumb. The sword should not move.

There is no one perfect grip. With practice, you will come to hold the sword slightly differently depending on what you want to do with it. Just as a learner driver grips the steering wheel, knuckles white from the tension, and an experienced driver just feels through their hands what the car is doing and responds effortlessly; so with swords.

Centres of Rotation

When cutting, the sword must turn around a particular point. That point is called the centre of rotation. The sword has a natural centre of rotation which you would see if you tossed the sword up in the air—it will spin around a particular point, usually a short way down the blade from the handle. (Don't try this, as coming down it's bound to hurt someone or something!) Many ways of striking take advantage of this natural rotation point. Others create an artificial centre of rotation, usually at the forefinger of the sword hand, in the middle of the blade, or at the pommel. For now, don't worry about it, but see if you can notice the point around which your sword is turning.

Natural Striking

Let's get started with a simple exercise that requires only you, a sword, and plenty of space.

Visualise a target in front of you, stand still with your feet apart, and swing your sword at it, without thinking too much about it. Occupy your thinking mind with noticing what the blow feels like.

Let the first blow swing forwards with enough relaxed vigour that it ends up swinging around to your opposite shoulder (so if it started on the right, it finishes on the left). Right now, I don't care about starting position, ending position, accuracy or anything else, except that the movement be comfortable and easy. Do it as fast or slow as you like.

A Jani starts with the sword on his right shoulder and **B** swings it forwards and **C** onto his left shoulder; **D** and back through the centre; **E** to his right shoulder.

Once this is comfortable, add a step. Start with the sword on your right shoulder, and your left foot forwards. As you swing from the right, step with your right foot. You are now right foot forwards with your sword on your left shoulder. Keep going. As you swing from the left, step with your left foot, swing from the right, step from the right. Let the sword swing from shoulder to shoulder, in a relaxed and easy manner.

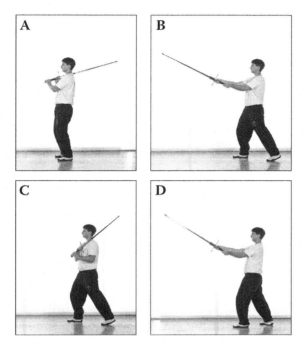

A Jani starts with the sword on his right shoulder and **B** swings it
forwards stepping with the right foot and **C** swings it onto his left
shoulder (no step); **D** and back to the centre.

Now let's look at the timing of the steps. Slow the swing down so
that you can see the point of maximum extension from the body.
Adjust your timing so that the stepping foot hits the floor at about
the same time as the sword reaches the point of maximum extension. Better that the sword is early than late.

Mandritto Fendente, Roverso Sottano
Now we begin with the most common blow in martial arts: a
forehand (*mandritto*) downwards blow (*fendente*). Continuing from
the natural striking drill above, let us prepare by getting the sword
onto our right shoulder, in a relaxed and comfortable way. How
you get into your starting position will determine what you can
do from it (because it affects which muscles are tense, and which

are relaxed). So, ideally get the sword onto the shoulder by swinging it into position, as in the previous drill. This is *posta di donna*. We will examine it in more detail later, but for now, just know that this is a guard position and move on.

From this position, a *mandritto fendente* is easy and natural. The sword is high and to the right: swing it forwards and it will fall low and to the left. If we follow Fiore's instructions, our sword will cleave the opponent in the jaw, rip through his chest leaving a bloody trail, and exit from their knee. At the moment of maximum extension, we are in *posta longa*, and if we follow the cutting path precisely, we will end up with the sword pommel against our left hip, the sword pointing down and to the left, and notice with pleased surprise that we are in a perfectly correct *posta di dente di zenghiaro*. (Note that *zenghiaro* with the sword is different to *zenghiaro* unarmed.) Turned into a drill:

1. Begin in *posta di donna destra* (on the right)
2. Throw the point of the sword towards *posta longa*, following with a pass forwards with the right foot
3. Allow the sword to drop down and through into *posta di dente di zenghiaro*. This should be one smooth motion, the sword passing through *posta longa* without stopping.

A Jani begins in posta di donna; B brings the sword forwards, tip first ...

C and strikes through posta longa into; **D** posta di dente di zenghiaro.

The descending force on impact comes from the rotation of the blade: the hand and sword drop only after contact with the target.

So, how do we get back up? It would be a shame to waste a movement, so push your point into *posta longa*, passing forwards with your left foot, and let the momentum of the movement (which happens to be a blow called *roverso sottano*) bring you back into *posta di donna destra*.

This lends itself to a walking drill: strike *mandritto fendente-roverso sottano* and back until you run out of space, then turn around and keep going.

For Left-handers:

Forehand (*mandritto*) and backhand (*roverso*) are the critical distinction to make here, so for you this drill will start in a left-side *posta di donna*, and go through to a right-side *dente di zenghiaro*, and back up.

A Left-handed, Jukka stands in posta di donna; B and begins his mandritto fendente; C and arrives in posta longa; D and allows the sword to fall into zenghiaro. Note that Jukka is not naturally left-handed, but senior students are expected to train everything both ways. Useful when the only left-hander at the photoshoot happens to be the photographer!

To recap this section: you now know three guards (*posta di donna destra*, *posta longa* and *dente di zenghiaro*) and two blows (*mandritto fendente* and *roverso sottano*). It is worth noting that as flow creates structure, and structure enables flow, if you find that your *dente di zenghiaro* doesn't look or feel right, change the exact path of the fendente to change the guard. Or if you find your fendente is a bit awkward, adjust *posta di donna* a bit. How? Try adjusting the swing from the left that got you there.

And On the Other Side ...

To strike a *roverso fendente* (backhand descending blow), let's first find *posta di donna sinestra* (left side woman's guard). This should not pose a challenge, as we just go back to our natural striking drill and swing the sword from right shoulder to left. We should note here that Fiore does not show the forward-weighted form of this guard anywhere, only the rear-weighted. But as we know that all guards can do a *volta stabile*, that is not a problem.

From *posta di donna sinestra* simply throw the point of the sword into *posta longa*, with a pass forwards, and allow the blade to swoosh through until your left hand connects with your left hip. This end position is called *tutta porta di ferro*, the guard of the whole iron door. So:

1. Begin in *posta di donna* sinestra
2. Strike *roverso fendente* into *posta longa*, passing forwards with the left foot
3. Allow the sword to drop through into *tutta porta di ferro*.

A Ken stands in posta di donna la sinestra;
B the sword goes forwards;
C and arrives in posta longa with a pass;
D and falls into tutta porta di ferro shown from the side and front.

We could allow the sword to swing through until it pointed behind us; that would be *coda longa*. It is correct to do so, but it takes more control to arrive in *tutta porta di ferro*, so I tend to require my students to do it this way.

So, we can now add three more guards to our collection: *donna* on the left, *tutta porta di ferro*, and *coda longa*. Of course, from either of the low guards, we can swing back up into *posta longa*, striking with the false edge. This creates the blow *mandritto sottano*. If we follow through to *posta di donna*, we have another walking drill.

A Ken is in tutta porta di ferro; **B** he sends his point towards posta longa;
C and arrives in posta longa with a pass.

With the false edge *sottani*, the hand is naturally rising from the low guard to *longa*. The blade does not rotate at all, as that would require you to drop the point before striking, which slows you down.

NOTE: taking the sword behind you (such as from *posta longa* into *posta di donna*) should ONLY be done either out of measure, or when there is no opponent (he's been killed by the blow, or you're practising on your own). Otherwise an alert opponent could stab you in the face as your sword is being swung out of his way.

Sword Guards (Poste) Used So Far

Now that we have been paying attention to our blows, it makes sense to give some time and space to the guard positions from whence they come and in which they finish. Often, slight changes to the guard position can make big changes to the ease of striking out of it. The guards form a critical element of the theoretical structure of the system, so deserve to be looked at in their own right.

Posta di Donna

The guard of the woman, which has the sword on the right shoulder. Of all the guards, this is by far the most frequently illustrated, and is one of the few that is shown on both sides, and both forward and rear-weighted. With the weapon on the right side of the body, it is *destra*, right side; with the weapon on the left, the guard is called *sinestra*, left side.

Guy stands in posta di donna destra, forward-weighted

This position can be something of a strain if it is held incorrectly, usually due to a twist in the back.

Keep your shoulders in line with your hips. I think of avoiding creases in my shirt. Note that the false edge rests on your shoulder (not the flat!) and that both hands remain comfortably curled around the grip.

Let's create it in all four possible forms: right or left foot forwards, weight forwards or back. To find the rear-weighted position, a *volta stabile* is all that's required:

Guy stands in *posta di donna destra*, rear-weighted

This is the most commonly illustrated version of the position. Note that the sword may be angled down your back, as a more relaxed variant.

Fiore says that *Posta di donna destra* can:

- Make all seven blows of the sword
- Defend against all seven blows
- Exchange the thrust.

To find the left side, forward-weighted variation, place the sword on the left shoulder and your right foot in front; to find the rear-weighted version, simply execute a *volta stabile*.

Note that in all the manuscripts, all illustrated instances of this side of the guard are shown rear- weighted, and with the sword about horizontal.

Fiore says *posta di donna sinestra* can:

- Defend and strike quickly
- Deliver great blows

- Break the thrust
- Traverse and enter the *zogho stretto* (more on that later).

Guy stands in posta di donna sinestra, forward-weighted.

Guy stands in posta di donna sinestra, rear-weighted.

Tutta Porta di Ferro

'The whole iron door.' Your sword is down, but not touching the floor, arms as relaxed as possible. Your weight should be as much as possible on your front, left, foot, and your hips turned forwards such that your right heel comes off the ground. This is the first guard in Fiore's group of twelve. So make sure it's comfortable, and mobile. To use this guard, you need to be able to step offline, and/or pass diagonally easily.

- Left foot forwards
- Weight on front foot
- Pommel on left hip
- Sword pointing 90° to the right.

Ken stands in posta di tutta porta di ferro.

Fiore says *tutta porta di ferro* requires a good sword that is not too long, and can:

- Wait in defence against any hand-held weapon
- Parry and pass, coming to the *strette* (close or constrained plays)
- Break the thrust
- Defend against any attack

Posta di Dente di Zenghiaro
The position of the wild boar's tooth (or tusk). The wild boar kills by ripping upwards with its tusks, and so does this guard. The primary action from here strikes upwards with the false edge or point. You can get to this position comfortably by simply passing into it from *tutta porta di ferro*, keeping your hands where they were in relation to your hips. The sword is now on the left, and pointed slightly to the left.

- Right foot forwards
- Weight on front foot
- Pommel on left hip
- Sword pointing forwards and a little left

Rear-weighted:

In the Getty manuscript this guard is also shown rear-weighted, so from the position above, do a *volta stabile*, leaving the sword where it is:

- Right foot forwards
- Weight on back foot
- Pommel on left hip
- Sword pointing forwards, in the middle.

This rear-weighted version is called *posta di dente di zenghiaro la mezana* (middle boar's tooth).

Joni stands in posta di dente di zenghiaro, forward weighted.

Joni stands in posta di dente di zenghiaro la mezana.

Fiore says *zenghiaro* can:

- Deliver thrusts, with or without stepping, and returning with a *fendente*
- Defends well against *zogho stretto*
- Strikes at an angle across the opponent's sword (i.e. parries).

Posta Longa

'Long guard.' As the name implies, it is the maximum sensible forwards extension of the sword (note, not the maximum possible). It is held thus:

- Left foot forwards
- Weight on the front foot
- Sword extended forwards.

Jan stands in posta longa

Note the angle between the sword and the right arm: the blade is not in line with the forearm. We will go through this guard with most strikes, either cut or thrust, so get used to it. Keep your shoulders down and relaxed, and your back upright. Note also that while Fiore illustrates it left foot forwards, as one of the middle guards (where the sword is in line with the centreline of the body) it can be held with either foot forwards.

Fiore says *posta longa* can:

- Test the opponent's guards to deceive them
- Use deception (more than the other guards)
- Thrust
- Avoid blows (i.e. avoid being parried).

Coda Longa

'Long tail.' Standing left foot forwards, we can swing the sword down and back, so it is extended behind us like a long tail.

- Left foot forwards
- Weight on the front foot
- Sword held behind and to the right.

Joni stands in posta di coda longa

Fiore says *coda longa* can:

- Thrust forwards
- Parry

- Strike
- Pass forwards with a *fendente*
- Enter into *zogho stretto* without fail
- Be good for waiting in
- Shift easily into other guards.

Now that you have some blows and guards, we should start making them useful. The most common use of a *mandritto fendente* is to attack people; the most common use of a *roverso sottano* is to parry. The primary goal of a parry is to beat aside the incoming attack, allowing you to strike safely. In a while we will look at the things that may go wrong, as the attacker anticipates your actions, but for now, let's take our *roverso sottano* from *zenghiaro* and use it to defend against a *mandritto fendente*. You can find this technique on p. 31 recto of *il Fior di Battaglia*.

A parry works by using a line of stability in the defending sword to exploit a line of instability in the attacking sword. You should use all the mechanical advantages available to you.

The sword itself is mechanically strong in the plane of the edge, and weak in the plane of the flat. Likewise, in *posta longa*, the edges are supported by the bones of the forearm, which are literally pointing in the same direction. The triangle formed by the swordsman's arms is also supporting the edge. However, there is practically nothing supporting the flats—he has no bone in that direction. When trying to control the opponent's sword, where possible use your strong, supported edge against his weak, unsupported flat. This also minimizes damage to your edge if you are using sharp swords (if you *need* this book, you should not yet be using sharps—put them away and go and get your blunts!). So, as we strike out of *zenghiaro*, we should aim to meet the attacker's sword with our false edge to his outside flat, middle to middle, and at as close to a 90° angle as possible.

Blades intersect as mandritto fendente (on the right) is parred by roverso sottano (on the left).

Let us set up our first defensive drill.[9] Remember, masks on, common sense engaged. It is critically important that you can trust your partner, and that he has developed sufficient control of the weapon that he can throw a gentle, slow, but accurate and in-measure blow to just stroke the mask as if it were made of eggshell. If you have any doubts about your or your partner's ability to do this safely, then go to the striking exercises on p. 127 and practise them to develop the necessary skills.

1. Wait in *zenghiaro* (so, right foot forwards), attacker starts in *donna* on the right
2. Attacker strikes with *mandritto fendente*
3. Parry by beating the incoming sword up and to the right, with a *roverso sottano* using the false edge, supporting the parry with an *accrescere fora di strada* (a step offline to the right with the front foot); this dramatically increases the degree to which the attack is beaten away
4. Strike back down the way you came, with *mandritto fendente*, bringing your left foot up a bit, to return to a normal guard position.

In practice, the *accrescere* is two foot movements—the front foot

---

9   For reasons that are lost in the mists of time, within the syllabus of my school this is the beginning of a set drill called "Second Drill". If you are looking for this action on our Syllabus Wiki, it will be under that title.

moves (the *accrescere* proper) and the back foot then moves up to reform the guard position, or passes, or the front foot is returned to its original position. In this drill, the parry begins a trifle before and continues during the movement of the right foot, and the riposte occurs as the left foot reforms the guard position.

A Joni (on right) waits in dente di zenghiaro, Juhani in posta di donna. **B** Juhani attacks with a mandritto fendente. Note the measure. **C** Joni beats Juhani's sword up and right, while making an accrescere right. **D** Finding Juhani open, Joni strikes a mandritto fendente.

Juhani's strike is shown completed; he repeats the blow for Joni to parry. In basic drills we usually require beginners to execute each step of the drill separately, one following the other. This is called "stepping the drill".

Left-handers should practise these pair drills as far as possible without modification. If paired together, two left-handers will simply create the mirror image of the right-handed form of the drill. But when paired cross-handed (one righty, one lefty), the attacker should still strike as they are comfortable doing (i.e.

mandritto), and the defender still parries from *dente di zenghiaro*. This entails a change to the way the edges will meet: follow the principle of beating his sword aside, and making a good cross on his blade, striking with your edge, and let nature take its course. In practice, a left-handed *roverso sottano* parrying a right-handed *mandritto fendente* looks like the following image:

A Joni waits left handed in zenghiaro, Juhani attacks as before;
B Joni parries, beating Juhani's sword up and left with his false edge.

It is of course possible to reverse roles, and have *dente di zenghiaro* attack *posta di donna*, and use the *mandritto fendente* as a parry. Feel free to play with this, but for reasons which will become clear I will address this action later.

Sword Handling Drills

When you use a sword, your brain gets used to it being there, and begins to treat it as an extension of your body. This process is essential, as it allows you to control the sword precisely. For a beginner, the sword is a heavy lump of metal that has to be moved from place to place; a restriction on movement. It makes life more difficult. For a swordsman, the sword is the means by which he expresses his will; it is a tool, a labour-saving device; with it you can hit much more effectively and from further away than you can without it. It makes life easier. The process of changing the sword from a burden to a tool can be drastically speeded up by playing with the sword. So every chance you get, pick one up and play with it. No set drill, no "practice", just swing it about, fiddle with it and have fun.

I have developed a series of handling drills designed to make the sword a live and responsive part of you. There are a couple detailed in *The Swordsman's Companion*, and several on the Syllabus Wiki. These are not strictly "Fiore" and would take up far too much space to describe in detail here, with photos etc., so I have left them out. You can find them at http://www.swordschool. com/wiki/index.php/Fiore_basic_syllabus.

Chapter Five

MORE STRIKES, MORE DEFENCES

As we have seen, defending ourselves from the end-point of a *mandritto fendente* blow (*dente di zenghiaro*) is quite straightforward. So how about from *tutta porta di ferro*, our preferred end point of a *roverso fendente*? This raises the opportunity to learn a new guard, because you have not yet seen the end point of a blow from the right that is aimed at an incoming sword. The position looks like this:

Posta Frontale
Frontal guard (also called the crown guard). This guard is the main position used for making parries from the right, so is shown with the left foot forwards. It is not so commonly used for fencing from, nor do we usually go into it from a left side guard. Find it like so:

- Start with your left foot forwards
- Weight on the front foot
- Sword held almost vertical
- Crossguard about level with your eyes
- True edge turned to the left side (so flat towards your opponent).

Note that for the parry to work, it must close the line, and so the guard is held to the left of your face, not in the middle.

Fiore says *frontale* can:

- Cross the opponent's sword
- Defend against high thrusts by crossing and passing out of the way

Guy in posta frontale

- Defend against low thrusts by beating them to the ground and passing out of the way
- Defend against thrusts by passing backwards and striking a *fendente* to the head finishing in *dente di zenghiaro* from whence you thrust again. (In practice this is done as a defence against a feint, where the crossing failed because the attacker avoided it)

Frontale is the best end- position for a rising parry from the right side, so let's use it like so:

1. Attacker ready in right side *posta di donna;* you wait in *tutta porta di ferro*
2. Attacker strikes, passing forwards with a *mandritto fendente,* aiming at your head.

That's the problem. Here's the usual solution (aka first and second plays of the second master of *zogho largo*):[10]

1. Attacker ready in right side *posta di donna;* you wait in *tutta porta di ferro*

---

10 Because the starting positions are the first two guards in Fiore's "12 guards of the the sword in two hands", within the syllabus of my school, this is the beginning of "First Drill". You will find it on the Syllabus Wiki under that name.

2. Attacker strikes with *mandritto fendente*, aiming at your head
3. Parry with *frontale*, meeting the middle of the attacker's sword with the middle of your own, edge to flat
4. The attacker's sword is beaten wide to your left, so pass away from it (to your right), striking with a *mandritto fendente* to the attacker's left arm, and thrusting to the chest.

This is the canonical form of the technique. With beginners lacking arm and chest protection, we often change this to a *roverso fendente* to the mask. This is the shortest line of attack from the *frontale* position, so it is very efficient, but it makes the attacker's basic counter very easy (see next chapter for details).

Ken waits in tutta porta di ferro for Ilpo's
mandritto fendente from posta di donna.

Ilpo strikes, mandritto fendente.

Ken uses frontale to parry Ilpo's strike.

Ken strikes over Ilpo's left arm while passing out of the way.

The attack has been parried, creating a safe opening to strike. The parry in this case is a cover, and the complete defence (cover and strike) is, in Fiore's terms, a remedy, literally a remedy to the problem of the attack.

We now have a defence from both right and left side guards dealing with a forehand blow; let's look at thrusts next.

The Thrusts

The principal difference between the cut and the thrust is timing the arrival of the point to the centre of the target. If the point is fully extended, and so has the centreline, before contact, it must be a thrust. If the point comes to the centre after contact, first contact must have been made by the edge, so it's a cut. It is critical that the sword is moving in the right direction: for the thrust to work, the sword should be pushed forwards in the direction of the point. To cut, the sword should be moving across the line of the blade, around a centre of rotation.

Thrust—point arrives online before contact.

Cut—point arrives in the centre after the edge strikes.

We already have a walking drill in which you cut up with the false edge from *dente di zenghiaro* and from *tutta porta di ferro*. That same action can be easily adapted to become a thrust—simply strike with the point. Let's have a look at some other guard positions that are also well adapted for the thrust.

Posta di Porta di Ferro la Mezana
The middle iron door. This guard has the sword in the middle of the line, with your weight on your front foot. It is shown right foot forwards.

* Right foot forwards
* Weight on front foot
* Sword held down and forwards, in the middle.

Auri in mezana porta di ferro.

In this position, and in *zenghiaro* and *tutta porta di ferro*, I have a sense of being on top of the sword, almost like holding a balloon under water. The sword wants to fly up, but my weight on it keeps it down. So, from the middle iron door, let the point fly forwards into an imaginary opponent's face, following it with a pass. We are again in *posta longa*.

Fiore says *porta di ferro la mezana* requires a long blade, and can:

- Deliver strong thrusts
- Beat attacks up and away from below, returning with a *fendente*
- Be difficult to break without coming to the *strette*.

Jan thrusts up the middle from porta di ferro la mezana to posta longa.

You can thrust from a forward-weighted *posta di donna*, but it is a little awkward to start with. However, thrusting from the rear-weighted version is very easy, as it allows us to get the point online by shifting to *posta longa* during the *volta stabile* and before the pass. So we can create a credible threat before committing to entering measure. This will become very useful later when we are practising the feint.

This can be done from both sides: try it from *donna sinestra*. Thrusting from a high guard is even easier if you start with the point forward: the perfect position for this is *posta di fenestra*, the window guard.

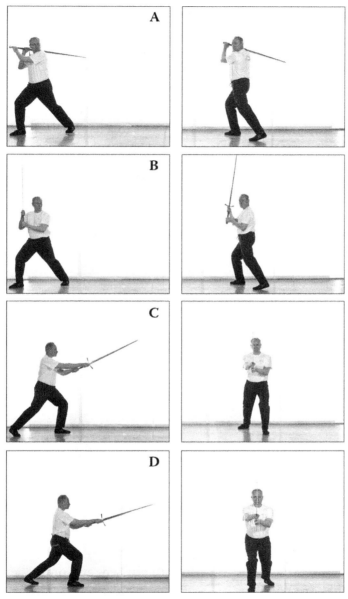

A Ilpo stands in rear-weighted posta di donna; B the strike begins;
C Ilpo arrive in posta longa; D and passes with his right foot.

Posta di Fenestra

The guard of the window. This position is a classic in swordsmanship, and analogues for it are found in most systems. It can cause trouble for beginners though, usually because they work too hard to get into it. With the sword, Fiore shows it only on the right side and rear-weighted (though in the pollax guards there is a left-side forward-weighted version, and he refers to a left side *fenestra* with the sword on folio 31r). Here it is on both sides:

A Ken in posta di fenestra, right side, rear-weighted.
B Ken in posta di fenestra, left side, rear-weighted.

- From *posta longa* do a *volta stabile*, keeping your point forward but drawing your hands back
- On the right side, the arms are crossed, and on the left side they are not
- Keep your shoulders down and relaxed
- The sword is horizontal, just above your eyes.

Many students find this tricky. One alternative that some find easier is to start in *posta longa*, at 135° from the line you want to be in. Get comfortable there. Then look over your shoulder into the line you want, and flip your sword point up and over, to point it in the right direction. From the shoulders down, rear weighted positions are basically the same as forward weighted ones, they just point in a different direction.

Fiore says *fenestra*:

- Is quick to defend and attack
- Is "Mistress of covers and strikes"
- Delivers strong thrusts
- Knows the break and exchange (of the thrust)
- Can pick a fight with any other guard, high or low.

Thrusting from *fenestra* is easy: just shove the point into *posta longa*, following the motion with a *volta stabile*, and pass.

A Ken is in fenestra, right side: **B** the thrust begins.

C the sword pulls Ken into posta longa; D and into a pass. E Ken is in fenestra, left side; F the thrust begins.

G the sword pulls Ken into posta longa.

Practise thrusting from all the guards you know. For this we have a game.

The Buckler Game

For this exercise we use a simple wooden buckler as a thrusting target. Your partner holds it in one hand (and wears a mask just in case), and offers it up for you to thrust at. His job is then to make you move about, offering the target at various heights, distances, and for decreasing lengths of time, making it difficult for you to get the thrust in. This should be calibrated so that you can hit it about three to four times out of five attempts. Less than that, he should slow down; more than that he should make things harder.

Guy coaching Ilpo with the buckler game.

Defending Against Thrusts: Breaking and Exchanging Thrusts

There are two fundamental techniques, repeated in various places in the manuscript, that form the basis of defence against thrusts. They are the *rompere di punta* (break the thrust) and the *scambiare di punta* (exchange the thrust). They can both be executed from *tutta porta di ferro*, so let's take it from there.

Breaking the Thrust:

The mechanics for this action are implied in Fiore's instructions: "catch his sword with a *fendente*, with your hands above and point below ..." I do this by keeping my pommel in place to start with, and rotating the sword around it, catching the incoming sword, then throwing the point forwards and to the left with the *accrescere*, following with the pass to step on the sword. Although Fiore shows stepping on the blade, to save wear and tear on our swords, it is okay to step just short of his point, which Fiore also shows. In either case, the beating down action must have finished before your passing foot arrives. You should try to throw his sword into the ground. From here you can strike, as Fiore instructs, "with the false edge, to the throat under his beard, returning with a *fendente* to the head or arms" thus:

1. Wait in *tutta porta di ferro;* the attacker is in *zenghiaro*[11]
2. Attacker enters with a thrust to your belly
3. Beat his sword down, stepping offline and passing across, keeping your sword forwards over his
4. Pick your point up and stroke the tip of the false edge across his throat, keeping your hands low, flicking the point up past his shoulder and across

---

11 This is suggested in the illustrations to this play (the 11th, 12th, and 13th plays of the second master of *zogho largo*, and following) which shows the attacker left foot forward— assuming he has passed in to attack, he must have started right foot forwards, perhaps in *zenghiaro*.

5. Continue the motion with a *roverso fendente* to the head. To do this, the point describes a half circle in the air after the throat is cut.

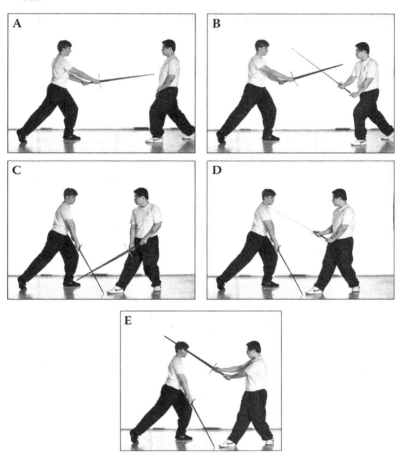

A Jan thrusts at Ken; **B** Ken parries while stepping offline to his left; **C** driving Jan's sword to the ground and passing such that he could step on Jan's blade; **D** and slices his false edge across Jan's throat; **E** whipping the sword around to strike a roverso to Jan's head.

The breaking of the thrust has also introduced us to a new type of blow—a horizontal cut, which we have seen done with the false edge from left to right (so, *roverso*). This cut is called a *mezano*, a middle blow, because its path lies between the *fendente* and the *sottano*. If we were to break the thrust from the left, we would finish by striking with a *mandritto mezano*. This is shown in the Pisani-Dossi manuscript, and is most easily done when breaking from *posta di donna*, rear-weighted, on the left:

1. Wait in *posta di donna* on the left, rear-weighted; the attacker is in *fenestra* on the right
2. Attacker enters with a thrust to your face
3. Beat his sword down, stepping offline and passing across, keeping your sword over his
4. Pick your point up and stroke the tip of the true edge across his throat, keeping your hands low, flicking the point up past his shoulder and across (*mandritto mezano*)
5. Continue the motion with a *mandritto fendente* to his head. To do this, the point describes a half circle in the air after the throat cut.

A Jukka waits in posta di donna la sinestra, Ville is in fenestra la destra;
B Ville attacks with a thrust; **C** Jukka parries with a roverso fendente;
D stepping off the line.

E driving Ville's sword to the ground; **F** and passes across towards Ville's sword; **G** and strikes a mandritto mezano to Ville's throat.

Fiore states that *posta di donna* on the left makes great blows, and *fenestra* "knows well the break" (i.e. you can break the thrust from there). So it must be correct to reverse the direction of the drill, and have *donna* attack *fenestra* with a thrust; *fenestra* breaks the thrust exactly as above from *tutta porta di ferro*. Can you think of any other guards that might break the thrust?

The Exchange of Thrusts

Fiore's instruction is to step out of the way and pass across and with your point high and your arms low, cross his sword and strike him in the face or chest (this is the ninth play of the second master of *zogho largo*).

1. Wait in *tutta porta di ferro*, attacker in the same guard.
2. Attacker thrusts to your belly
3. Pick up your point and cross his sword (middle to middle, edge to flat), hands stay low

4. Step your front (left) foot out of the way (to the left—this pushes his point further away from you)

5. And pass across (so, diagonally left), thrusting to his face (no need to lift your hands: keep them low!).

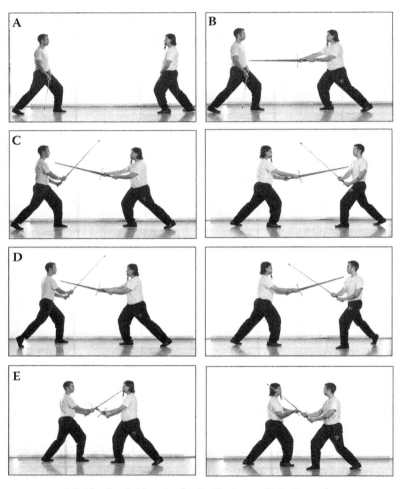

A Jukka (on left) waits for Joni's thrust; B Joni attacks;
C Jukka parries, D while stepping off the line;
E and strikes, passing across while thrusting into Joni's face..

Do this in one smooth motion: it feels like a simple strike that happens to collect his attack. But beware—it is critically important to make sure of your cover before passing in. Otherwise you get hit.

Fiore provides for the possibility that your thrust might miss so in the next play, he has us pass again (with the left foot in the same direction) while reaching over with our left hand to grab the opponent's sword between his hands, and strike.

A Jukka reaches over and grabs Joni's handle; B and lifts while bearing down on the sword and passing again; C leaving Joni hopelessly off balance.

If we suspect that the thrust may be too strong to exchange against safely, for instance because it begins on the attacker's left side and so must be pushed all the way across our centre, we must then commit to a much stronger defence, and beat his thrust to the ground, as we saw previously in "Breaking the thrust".

Counterattacking with a Cut

As we have seen in the exchange of thrusts, it is possible to parry and strike with a single motion of the sword. This kind of action is called a counterattack. It is of course possible to do this with a cut (Fiore refers to *contrapunte*, counter-thrusts, and *contrataglie*, counter-cuts, on folio 27v). The most common, and easy, of these is to use a *mandritto fendente* to defend against your opponent's *mandritto fendente*, like so:

1. You and the attacker are both ready in *posta di donna destra*
2. Attacker strikes with *mandritto fendente*, aiming at your mask
3. Counterattack with a *mandritto fendente* half blow, aiming to meet the middle of the attacker's sword with the middle of your own, stepping diagonally right with your right foot (*passo fora di strada*)
4. Your left foot follows around behind you, leaving you facing diagonally into the attacker's left side
5. As your point arrives on the attacker's mask.[12]

The defence against this is to parry the counterattack by redirecting the attack to close the line.

6. As your sword approaches his, the attacker redirects to parry it, binding your point away from his face. From here he can strike.

This drill is expanded on at length in Chapter 10, so please practise it until it is comfortable. As a general rule, like counters like. So you can try counterattacking with *roverso fendente* against *roverso fendente*, and so forth.

---

12 This action is for all intents and purposes identical to the Liechtenauer system's *meisterhau*, "*Zornhau ort*".

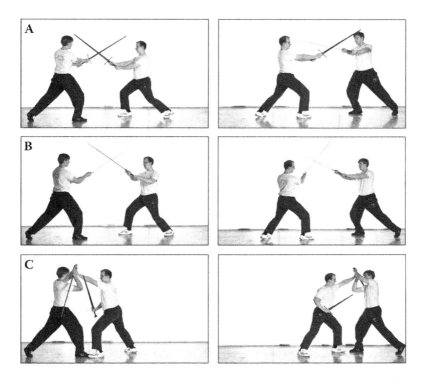

A Mikko has attacked; Jan counterattacks, passing out of the way; **B** Mikko parries Jan's counterattack; **C** Mikko enters, grabbing Jan's hilt.

Recapping this chapter, we have learned:

- Thrusts, from high and low guards
- Three new guards: *frontale*, *fenestra* and *mezana porta di ferro*
- Three defences from *tutta porta di ferro*: a parry with *frontale* against a *mandritto fendente*; the exchange of thrust, and the breaking of the thrust
- Breaking the thrust from *posta di donna sinestra*
- The *mezani* blows, *mandritto* and *roverso*
- Counterattacking with *mandritto fendente*.

Chapter Six

More Strikes, and More Guards

Now that you have the basics of striking, and can defend against those strikes, it makes sense to spend some time deepening your understanding of how strikes work and what you can do with them. The striking mechanics shown in *Il Fior di Battaglia* are very specific. Where in *The Swordsman's Companion* I tried to include all the possible striking variations compatible with Fiore's art, here we have only dealt with the ideal strikes that he describes, with reference to the context in which they are supposed to be applied. Fiore describes a total of eleven blows of the sword: six cuts and five thrusts. For reasons of style, he refers to the seven blows, which are the six cuts and the thrust. (Seven is a much easier number to remember things by than 11.) The six cuts are *mandritto* or *roverso* (forehand or backhand—in modern Italian, *diritto* and *rovescio*), *fendente* (descending), *sottano* (ascending), and *mezano* (middle—i.e. horizontal). The five thrusts are: from above, forehand and backhand; from below, forehand and backhand; and up the middle.

For our current purposes, the guards are simply the beginning, middle and end positions of the blows. We create Fiore's guards by making the blows in the correct lines, as naturally as possible. Every blow is a transition from one guard to another. At the moment the blade strikes, we are usually in *posta longa* (long position).

Fiore clearly illustrates the paths of the blows, on p. 23 recto.

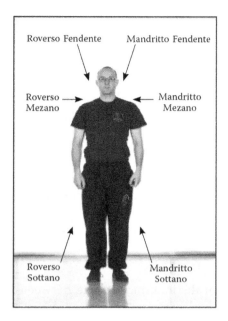

Lines of the blows

How you strike is the same in every case: your sword hand goes from the starting guard to the extended guard (usually *longa*) in the straightest possible line. No deviations, no curves. The point is to hit first, not to hit as hard as possible. Once you have whacked someone in the head with a reasonably fast-moving, four foot bar of sharpened steel, you will probably have the luxury of hauling off to make the second blow as hard as you like, because he is in no condition to do anything about it. But any slight increase in the time the blow takes to go from start to impact dramatically increases the opponent's ability to counter it.

In basic training, the first blow almost never connects unless the defender chooses to allow it (for whatever training purposes). At a more advanced level, that changes as you learn to manipulate your opponent's perception of when the blow will arrive. The first and simplest of these tricks is to strike without the slightest warning—eliminating any telegraph of your intention. No twitch of an eyebrow, no slight whitening of the knuckles, no bunching of the shoulders, just an immediate transition from where you are to where you want to go. This requires three things:

- An accurate, relaxed guard position in which to start
- An absolutely direct extension of the sword hand towards the target.
- Efficient, clean mechanics.

Practise your blows in the mirror, imagining how you would counter the vicious attacker you see before you: it's a great way to spot flaws and openings in your attacks.

Full and Half Blows

There is a critical distinction to make between blows that finish with the point in line (i.e. in *posta longa*) and blows that follow through to a low guard. For maximum defensiveness, leave your point in line (this is a half blow). For maximum striking power, cut through: this is a full blow. Later Italian swordsmanship systems make a core tactical distinction between these two types, and it is implied in the structure of Fiore's Art too. For our modern purposes, it is almost never necessary and seldom advisable to use a full blow, as we neither want to break our training partners nor do we want to leave ourselves open after the strike. However, they are a key component of the art in its original form, and so should be practised. There are few things in life as satisfying as finishing a fencing match with a full blow on the opponent, perfectly controlled, clean, clear, and done at a time when he has no hope of taking advantage of the opening line it creates.

With practice it is possible to cut and thrust from most guards, but some are clearly better adapted for certain strikes than others. Play with them, and make sure that in every case, with every blow, the action is the smoothest, shortest possible motion from the guard you start in to the guard you finish in. The sword hand always moves in a dead straight line. For example, when cutting from *posta di donna* to *posta longa*, the sword hand just goes straight forwards; the rotation of the blade around it provides the downward component. If cutting through to *dente di zenghiaro*, as the arm reaches full extension the hand just drops, like throwing a stone on the end of a string. When the string is fully extended, the stone falls in an arc.

Putting the Blows Together

Now would be a good time to revise and practise all the strikes you know so far. Here is a customisable drill to refresh your memory. In my school's basic syllabus it is known as "The Cutting Drill". It is made up of two parts: the first is a fairly simple routine that beginners can pick up quite quickly; the second is a set of applications from the treatise. Let's start with part one:

The Cutting Drill, Part One:

1. Begin in *posta di donna destra*, left foot forwards
2. Cut a full *mandritto fendente* through *posta longa* to *dente di zenghiaro*, passing (finish right foot forwards)
3. Cut a *roverso sottano* to *posta longa*, with the false edge, passing (finish left foot forwards)
4. Go to *posta di donna destra* (no step)
5. Cut a half *mandritto fendente* to *posta longa*, passing (finish right foot forwards)
6. Go to *posta di donna sinestra* (no step)
7. Cut a full *roverso fendente* to *tutta porta di ferro*, passing (finish left foot forwards)
8. Cut a *mandritto sottano* to *posta longa*, false edge, passing (finish right foot forwards)
9. Go to *donna sinestra* (no step)
10. Cut a half *roverso fendente* to *posta longa*, passing (finish left foot forwards)
11. Bring the sword back to *posta di donna destra* (no step).

Once the basic choreography is down, try the following variations:

- At step 3, the *roverso sottano* could also be a rising thrust, or a parry (especially if you use an *accrescere* offline instead of a pass)
- At step 8, instead of the *mandritto sottano*, you could also cut true edge to *frontale*
- (a parry) and strike into *posta longa*. Or indeed do the break or exchange of thrust.
- You will have noticed that there aren't a lot of thrusts—so try making every transition into *posta longa* a thrust instead of a cut
- Try the drill in this same form using *fenestra* instead of *posta di donna*, using cuts or thrusts to enter *posta longa*.

This drill can and should be customised to suit your needs and interests. Having trouble with cutting from *fenestra*? Then emphasise that variation. Can't get enough of lovely *frontale*? Then see what guards you can usefully get into it from- make the blows a parry-riposte combination instead. The guards you already know are: *posta di donna, tutta porta di ferro, dente di zenghiaro, posta longa, posta di fenestra, posta frontale, posta di coda longa, porta di ferro mezana.*

Of the twelve guards that Fiore would have us know, there are only two left. This is because he shows *zenghiaro* twice (forward and back weighted) and *donna* twice (left and right sides). For the sake of completeness, let's have a look at the last two: *posta breve* and *posta di bicorno*.

Posta Breve

Short guard. Fiore explicitly states that this guard is mostly used when in armour, moving around our opponent looking for an opening to thrust into. As such, we don't use it terribly often, but slight variations on this position form part of several techniques, such as the exchange of thrust and the *roverso mezano*, which you have already seen.

- Left foot forwards
- Pommel held against the body, in the centreline
- Point up and angled forwards.

Ville stands in posta breve.

Fiore says *breve*:

- Requires a long blade
- Is deceitful
- Probes the opponent for an opportunity to thrust
- Is better used in armour.

The guards *porta di ferro la mezana, posta longa*, and *posta breve* are referred to by Fiore as 'point in line' guards (*"guardie che stano in punta"*, literally "guards that stand in the point"). As the sword is in the middle, either foot can lead, and indeed you should practise these passing from one to the other, so either foot is forwards. This is especially the case for *posta longa*, which you know as the striking point of an attack from either side.

So, all that remains is the tricksy and elusive *posta di bicorno* ...

Posta di Bicorno
The two- horned guard. This guard is fundamentally a variation of *posta longa*, with an adjustment to the grip such that instead of supporting the edges, we support the flats. This makes thrusts made with this position much harder to parry. This guard has excited

much debate, and I have written up my interpretation of it in my article *Finding Bicorno* (available free online). You can find it like so:

- Start in *posta longa*
- Turn your right hand around the grip until your forearm is in line with the flat;
- Bring your hand in a bit until your left hand touches your right wrist;
- Bring your elbows in towards each other.

Guy in bicorno

If you have difficulty finding the grip, try holding the sword normally, and pushing the edge near the tip against the floor—nice and solid. Now, test the flex of your sword by shifting it around and bending the flat (gently!). Notice what you did to your grip. The sword is rotated around in your hand so you can push in the line of the flat. That's the essence of the *bicorno* guard.

A Ken bends the flat of his sword on the floor; **B** Guy applies pressure to the flat of Ken's sword: the blade bends, Ken's hands don't move.

Fiore says *bicorno*:

- Stands so closed that the point always stays in the middle of the line, and can do what *longa* does, so:
- Tests the opponent's guards to deceive them
- Uses deception (more than the other guards)
- Thrusts
- Avoids blows (i.e. avoids being parried).

The Difference Between Thrusting with *Bicorno* and *Longa*?

The mechanical difference between *longa* and *bicorno* comes from the shift in the grip, and a slight retraction of the hands. If we contrast the lines of stability between *bicorno* and *longa* (cf *The Duellist's Companion* pp. 85–7, and the forthcoming Volume Three of this series for details of the testing process) we see the following:

	Longa	Bicorno
True edge	Supported	Unsupported
False edge	Supported	Unsupported
Flat inside	Unsupported	Supported
Flat outside	Unsupported	Supported
Point	Supported	Supported

This reversal of the stability properties of the positions comes from the alignment of the blade relative to the forearm: in *posta longa*, the edges are in line with the bones of the forearm; because of the turn of the sword, in *bicorno* the flats, especially the inside flat, are supported by the forearm.

This reversal is so extreme that if we apply enough force to bend the sword by ninety degrees, the swordsman's structure is unaffected. Contrast with what happens to the swordsman's hands when *longa* is pressured in the same way:

A Ken checks that he is supporting the edges;
B Ken in longa, Guy applies pressure. Ken's sword is moved out of the way.

Due to the closing up of the space between the hands when in the thrust becomes much harder to parry: you have to literally bend the sword out of the line. This makes *bicorno* not only devastatingly fast to thrust with, but very hard to parry; literally, "the point stays in the middle of the line" *despite your opponent's best efforts to move it.*

The instability of the edges also means that they are very mobile; any attempt to break the thrust naturally creates a yielding action in the blade, and makes this position very good to feint with: as *longa* avoids blows (avoiding a blow is the same thing as avoiding a parry; the blow to the blade is the *rebattere*, a beating parry common to this system), so does *bicorno*; start in *donna*, throw the point out to *bicorno*, as your opponent parries, dip your point around their blade, and walk your thrust in. (We will drill this action later.)

It is far less sensible to cut with *bicorno*—the same stable properties of the flats have been stolen from the edges, so making them much less able to resist the impact exerted by the target on the sword.

So, let's find *bicorno* from *posta di donna*:

1. Stand in *posta di donna*, rear-weighted. Ideally, get there with a relaxed blow

2. Flick the point of your sword forwards, allowing the rotation to shift the handle in your grip, into *bicorno*
3. Supporting the action with a *volta stabile*.

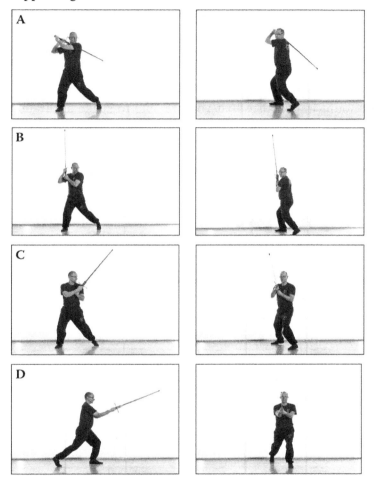

A Guy starts in posta di donna rear-weighted; **B** the point flicks up;
C the sword pulls Guy into a volta stabile;
D the volta stabile is complete and Guy is in posta longa.

You can also get there easily from *coda longa*. I like to do this as a combination starting in *posta di donna sinestra*:

1. Start in *posta di donna la sinestra*
2. Throw a fast *roverso fendente*, passing, all the way through to *coda longa*
3. Without stopping, flick the point forwards into *bicorno*, and pass.

Time to Hit Things

This chapter has been mostly about striking mechanics. It is of paramount importance that you are able to strike accurately and hard, without damage to yourself. In friendly sparring and pair drills, it is of course also vital that you can hit gently without damage to anyone. The two main tools we use to practise these skills are the tyre and the pell.

Hitting the Tyre

An ordinary car tyre, held by a helpful partner, is an ideal striking target as it absorbs some, but not all, of the impact. You can hit it with absolutely full-force without endangering the person holding it (unless you miss), and while it gives some shock back into the sword and your hands, much of the force is taken by the elastic give of the tyre. Every target hits back- every action has an equal and opposite reaction. If your technique is correct, you can direct the returning energy down into the ground. If not, the tyre will bounce your sword up and off. I recommend adding a strip of duct tape as a more precise aiming point. When you hit the tyre, the energy going into it should be absorbed by the tyre (and your partner). You should feel almost nothing. Start gently, standing still, and work your way up adding speed and power slowly. Then try adding footwork, such as striking with a pass.

Your body knows that to hit hard, it should step first, and strike with the rotation of the hips. This will give you maximum power, but get you killed in a sword fight. It is critically important to remember that the tyre is not waiting with a sword to kill you, and therefore will let you get away with wildly incorrect timing- you can step into measure and *then* strike. You and your partner should watch for this.

Jukka holds the tyre for Ville to strike.

Using the Pell

The pell is a post, often with a crossbeam, fixed upright for you to cut and thrust at. Try the following exercises:

- Pick one blow, and see how hard and fast you can strike at the pell without touching
- Repeat with multiple strikes (use your imagination!)
- Strike fast, but stroke the pell gently on a marked spot (about as hard as you would like to be hit in freeplay). See how hard and fast that really is
- Repeat with multiple strokes

The 99 strikes exercise: Make 100 cuts at the pell, without touching it. Every time you touch it, the counter resets to zero. So if you touch on strike 99, you go back to the beginning …

- Choose a specific strike, and approach the pell from far away, moving smoothly and without stopping with blows from guard to guard: see if you can arrive in measure with your sword in the right place to launch the pre-arranged strike. This is harder than it sounds.

The same caveat applies as with the tyre—be careful to time your strikes to land a fraction before your passing foot touches the ground.

Juhani strikes at (but doesn't touch) the pell.

Chapter Seven

COUNTER-REMEDIES, THEIR COUNTERS, AND IMPROVING THE GUARDS

Having practised defending from the left and the right against cuts and thrusts, you should have a pretty good idea what to expect from your opponent when you attack. Understanding the opponent's options when you launch an attack makes successful counter-remedies possible. The "universal" counter- remedy is found in the mounted combat section, the eighth play of the master of *coda longa* on horseback provides "a counter to ALL the plays that come before": as the opponent parries, "turn your sword and strike him in the face with the pommel".

1. Defender waits in *zenghiaro* (so, right foot forwards), while you begin in *donna destra*
2. You attack with a *mandritto fendente*
3. Defender parries by beating your sword up and to his right
4. Allow your blade to be beaten across, keeping your hands to your right. This covers against the defender's riposte
5. Let go of the handle with your left hand, extending your left arm, and pass in with the left foot
6. Wrap up both of the defender's arms, leaving him helpless for the pommel strike. You may also present the point of the sword.

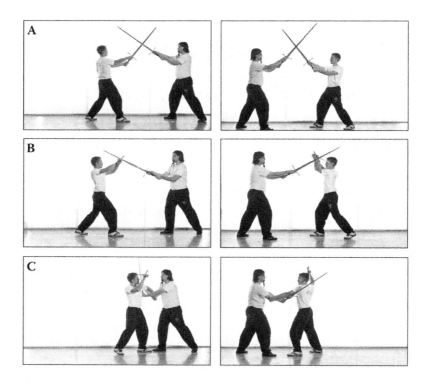

A Juhani (no beard) has attacked; Joni (with beard) has parried from zenghiaro; B Juhani turns his sword to cover Joni's strike and; C wraps Joni's arms with his left arm, immobilising him for the pommel strike.

We have, then, a three-step drill: the attack, the remedy, and the counter-remedy. Or, cut, parry, wrap. This should be practised step by step, so: cut; cut, parry riposte; cut parry riposte, wrap and pommel strike. 1, 1-2, 1-2-3; 1, 1-2, 1-2-3.

This is because each technique is designed to work against a committed attack of some sort, but it is very common in training for people to "take turns". If you know your cut is supposed to be parried, you can forget to cut properly. It is absolutely crucial that you execute every action as if you believed it would work or else you are not only practising poor technique, but also failing to provide your partner with a proper stimulus for his response, in effect training him to react wrongly. Practising by stepping the drill ensures that every action is concluded properly at least once, and, critically, sets up the problem for the next technique to solve.

If you feel your partner is fluffing the riposte because he "knows" the pommel strike is coming, leave it out. And watch him catch himself in a critical error. This is helpful partnering. Once the basic choreography is clear, randomize the degree to which the drill is taken. For example, defenders decide at random not to parry and see if the original attack would actually make contact. You'll be amazed how often people's expectations overwhelm their conscious decisions. It is quite common for the defender, in drill, knowing his strike will be countered, to omit the strike and pull his arms back. If that happens, just push a little with your left hand on his elbow, and be a little more vigorous in your pommel strike. He will hopefully soon learn to put some intention behind his actions.

Fiore shows two solutions to the problem of being wrapped up like this. Both of them require you to act before the wrap is fully in place, and long before you are smashed in the face with the pommel or stabbed with the point. The first, and most important as it is repeated in several variations in *Il Fior di Battaglia*, is to counter-lock with the *ligadura sottana.* Treat the incoming left arm wrap as an attack, and raise your sword arm to collect his left elbow, executing another *accrescere* in the same direction as before, then turn with a *volta stabile* to place him in the lower lock (*ligadura sottana*).

1. As the attacker enters extending his left arm
2. Collect his elbow with your right wrist
3. Break his structure with your step
4. And turn into the lock (carefully!)

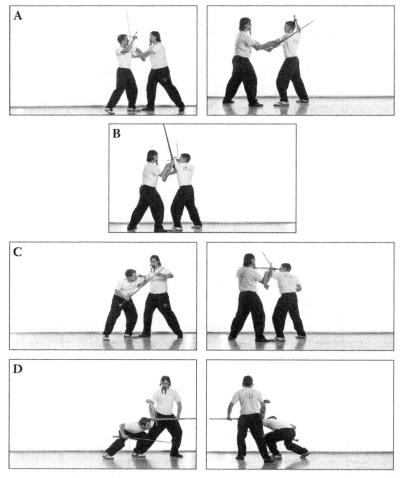

A Juhani reaches over Joni's arms; **B** Joni lifts Juhani's elbow; **C** Joni grabs his blade with his left hand and; **D** applies the lock.

For more detail on how to apply joint locks, refer to pp. 37–39 of *The Medieval Dagger*.

When practising in a cross-handed pair, you will find that the arms aren't there to be wrapped, so instead push the elbow.

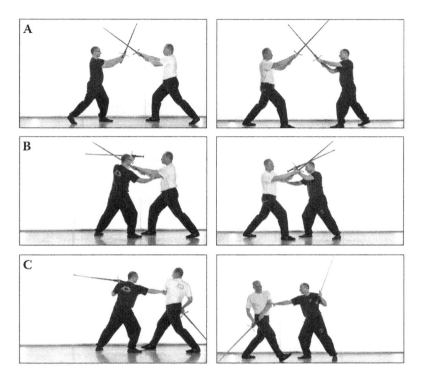

A Guy (left-handed) attacks Ilpo, who has parried; **B** Guy enters
to push Ilpo's elbow; **C** turning him so he cannot strike.

This is countered by pushing the attacker's sword away and
thrusting from underneath.

Ilpo intercepts Guy's sword hand, turning him to strike.

We should notice that the same principle can be applied against a
defender parrying from the right side such as from *tutta porta di*

ferro. Note that because we are now on the other side, we can't envelope both of the defender's arms under our left, but the outside of his elbow is available to be pushed.

1. Be ready in right side *posta di donna*. Defender waits in *tutta porta di ferro*
2. Attack with a *mandritto fendente*, aiming at his head
3. Defender parries with *frontale*, meeting the middle of your sword with the middle of his own, edge to flat
4. Allow the point of your sword to be beaten wide. Keeping your sword hand up and forwards, allow that momentum to turn your sword around, creating a natural cover against the defender's strike, and presenting the pommel forwards
5. Pass in immediately, using your other hand to control your opponent's elbow
6. Strike the defender's mask (gently!) with your pommel.

A Ilpo has attacked Ken, who parries; **B** Ilpo enters, covering Ken's strike;

C and pushes Ken's elbow and pommel strikes.

Happily, Fiore also provides a specific counter-counter-remedy to this, in the ninth play of the master of *coda longa* on horseback, in which as the pommel strike comes in, he simply raises his sword to deflect it, and executes a pommel strike himself.

1. Set up the previous drill
2. As you parry and the point of the attacker's sword is beaten wide (end of step three in the previous drill) he enters with the pommel strike
3. Your strike after the parry fails against the attacker's cover
4. As his pommel strike comes in, lift your hands, directing the attack off to the side, and strike the attacker in the face (also gently!).

Ken lifts his sword, bending his elbow, to
deflect Ilpo's pommel strike and place his own.

A cross-handed pair will find that there should be the opportunity for the attacker to wrap the arms, but the normal counter to a wrap as shown above in the first set of drills doesn't work quite right here. So instead, step out of the way and push the attacker's sword up and away with your off-hand.[13]

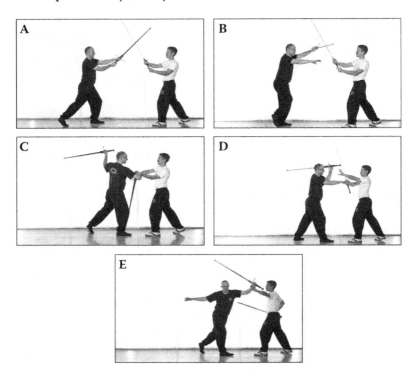

A Guy has attacked left-handed; Juhani parries from tutta porta di ferro;
B Guy covers and is entering; C Guy wraps Juhani's arms and strikes;
D Juhani intercepts Guy's entry and E pushes him off balance to strike.

Tactical Analyses of the Guards

As we saw in the previous chapters, the guards form the waypoints of the system. They are places to start from, places to finish in, and places to pass through. Small changes in position can have major consequences in action.

Any position you find yourself in can be considered a guard if you understand its tactical and technical properties. Slavishly

---

13 These two four-step sequences are set drills in my school's syllabus: First drill, beginning with *tutta porta di ferro*, Second drill, beginning with *zenghiaro*. You can find videos of them on the Syllabus Wiki.

copying a position from the treatise is useless unless you have some idea of what the position is for, what openings it leaves and what strengths it possesses. So let's take a look at the critical components of a position held with the sword. They are:

- Which foot is leading
- Which side the sword is held on
- Where the weight is (forwards or back)
- The position of the sword (forwards, back, left right, high, low etc.)
- How the sword is held
- All of the above, relative to your opponent.

Let's start with the sword. The further away your sword is from the centre, the longer it takes to get there, but the harder it will strike or parry when it does finally make contact. This is because the further your sword travels, the more time it has to accelerate, so the faster it is moving when it arrives. Which part of your sword is supported by the grip—edge or flat? This will determine what you can hit with. (The point should always be supported.)

Whose sword is closer to the centre—yours or your opponent's? If you can get to a position where his sword is too far away from the centre to parry in time, you can hit him easily.

Now the feet: the position of your front foot relative to your opponent determines how close to him you can get with a pass. The position of your back foot relative to your opponent determines how far away from him you can get with a pass back, and how long a pass forwards will take, because it determines how far the foot has to go from start to finish.

The placement of your weight: the main target is your head, which is directly above your centre of mass (or should be!). So the position of your weight relative to your feet determines both how far your weight has to travel when striking your opponent, and how far your opponent has to travel when striking you.

Every guard position is a specific set of compromises, such as:

- A fast pass forwards at the expense of starting with your head closer to your opponent
- A harder strike at the expense of starting with your sword held back and to the side
- Making your opponent travel farther to reach you, at the expense of a longer and therefore slower pass forwards for you
- Keeping your sword closer to the centre, to close the line quicker, at the expense of having less power available when you get there.

Let's take a concrete example of two guards that are often blurred together by beginners: *tutta porta di ferro* and *coda longa*. They both are held left foot forwards, with the weight on the front foot. This allows for a fast and easy pass forwards with the right foot. The sword is held either behind and to the right (*coda longa*) or pointing directly to the right (*tutta porta di ferro*). A strike from either guard usually ends in *posta longa*. If we take a thrust from below from *coda longa*, we see that we pass almost exactly through *tutta porta di ferro*, so it must take longer to do.

Likewise, when parrying from either guard, we would often use *frontale*. Measuring the distance from one to the other, we see that again, *coda longa* strikes harder but takes longer. This means that we must start the movement earlier to get there at the right time (before the attack hits us).

The "correct" choice of guard then is very often a function of measure. The farther away you are from the opponent, the safer it is to keep the sword farther back or offline.

It is necessary to study all the guards that your opponent may use against you, so that you may understand their tactical significance. At an advanced level, you might convey the appearance of being too far from the centre to defend in time, or being too far back to strike quickly, and take advantage of your opponent's misjudgment of your position. Developing this skill of analysing the tactical elements of a position is also crucial to your success when faced with an opponent who is either trained in a different system, or is using non-standard positions. What can I do from here?

Guy in a very non-standard guard

At the beginning of the sword in two hands material, Fiore shows us various ways of gripping the sword: for throwing, for defence with one hand, for executing an extended thrust, for fighting in armour, and finally back to *posta di donna*, with a sword, and with a boar-hunting sword held like an axe.

A Joni stands to throw the sword; Guy has the sword in one hand. **B** Joni holds his pommel to thrust further; Guy holds the sword by blade and handle, for armoured combat. **C** Joni in forward weighted posta di donna, "normal grip"; Guy holds the sword by the blade, in rear-weighted posta di donna.

This section illustrates the different ways of holding the sword, so that we can a) use them and b) recognise them if our opponent is about to try something tricky. Every one of these positions has a specific set of tactical and technical attributes, some of which Fiore is kind enough to explain in detail. For a complete translation and explanation of Fiore's instructions, you can refer to my article *Technical and Tactical Notes on the Longsword Guards of Il Fior di Battaglia*, available free online. For present purposes, you first need to know exactly how to hold each position, and what you will generally be able to do from it. It is critically important that you structure any guard such that you can do what you intend from there without adjusting the position in any way. For example, if your fingers are open on the hilt, and you have to close them before you can strike, that's a mistake. If you wish to pass immediately, but your weight is too far back on your rear foot and you have to shift it forward before your back foot can move, that's a mistake. The technical drills so far should have given you an idea of what you should be able to do from a given position, and so some insight into the precise details of the guards.

The way you enter a position affects which muscles are tense or relaxed while in the position. If this is an unfamiliar concept, try holding a squat, with your hips level with your knees. Use a stopwatch to see how long it takes until it hurts, first when you lower yourself into the position, and secondly when you drop past it and then come up into the same position. Usually, people find that dropping into it makes it easier to hold, as the muscles that are keeping you up are more relaxed, and therefore not working as hard when you get there, so they can keep working for longer. Try it and see.

It is a good idea to practise entering all the guards in as many different ways as make sense, as this gives you further insight into when you should be in what position. To begin with, practising holding the guards may make you static and stiff, so intersperse guards practice with some vigorous moving around.

Let's finish this chapter with my secret weapon when it comes to learning structure. This is the Stability Drill.

The Stability Drill

You will need a wall clock that has a second hand clearly visible, and ideally a mirror to check details of your position.

1. Start in *posta di donna*. Note the time on the clock. Consciously and deliberately relax all unnecessary tension. Arms, shoulders, back and legs are all probably doing more work than necessary. Your body won't allow you to collapse in a puddle on the floor, so anywhere that you feel tense, try to let go.
2. Relax and sink into the position until you feel a better, more stable guard has been formed. Pause for a few seconds. Note how long you've been in the guard for.
3. Strike into *posta longa*, return to donna and strike back into *longa*, with or without a pass as you like. It's generally easier to pass, as it puts the primary strain on the other leg.

4. In *posta longa*, note the time, and start the relaxation process again. You may well feel it in the arms and shoulders. Try to push the point forwards, and imagine the sword being dragged away from you, so you are comfortably stretched out behind it.

5. Allow the sword to lead you into the next guard; perhaps *zenghiaro*, as the end of the blow, or volta stabile back to fenestra. Repeat the movement back and forth, and relax into the new guard.

Continue this process, noting how long you are usefully able to be in these positions. Stop when you are getting tired or bored. The next time you train, see if you can relax more, and so be able to sustain the positions for longer. The point is to establish a more efficient physical structure for the positions, and the movements between them, so that every bone is in the right place, reducing the muscular effort needed to hold the position, so your muscular strength is available for generating power in the strike. This also helps with any flexibility issues, allowing stretched muscles to relax and lengthen, and builds up the strength of your core muscular support.

I find about 60 seconds in each position, and doing this exercise for about 10 minutes three times a week, is enough to generate steady improvement in power generation, stability, and flow. Ideally, when holding a position (say, *posta longa*), the only sense of tension and muscular effort is in the thigh of the weighted leg. This usually takes about three to six weeks of regular practice.

Afterwards, you should feel energised and relaxed, ready to take on any opponent. If this is not the case, make sure you are not overdoing it, and make sure you are constantly trying to let go of tension, rather than to exert effort to hold the positions.

Chapter Eight

COUNTERS TO THE BREAK, THE SWORD IN ONE HAND, AND EXPLOITING MISTAKES

Countering the Exchange

D eliberately drawing your opponent's exchange of the thrust is very risky, as his parry and strike happen almost simultaneously. However, if it happens, you should have already figured out that closing the line with a turn of your sword and entering with a pommel strike should (according to Fiore) work. By entering with the thrust, you seriously limit your ability to bind the sword (more on this in the next chapter), so yielding is the option most likely to succeed.

Counter to the Break, Option One: Feint

We can take advantage of the fact that the rather large binding action that the defender uses to drive the attacker's sword to the ground makes him more than usually vulnerable to a feint. The feint is a threatening action that looks like an attack, which draws a parry in order to strike on the other side, without making contact with the parry. Using the feint is not terribly common in this system: Fiore doesn't include a single feint as a play anywhere, though he does refer to them in the descriptions of some of the guards. There is one play that follows the same logic as a feint, the *punta falsa* on fol 27v, but there Fiore explicitly tells us to "strike lightly on the sword", so it is not technically a feint as I am using the term. The *punta falsa* itself will be covered in the next volume (due out in 2016). Feints can be risky: the defender might hit you while you're hitting him if you fail to close the line.

1. Start in *zenghiaro*, the defender waits in *porta di ferro*
2. Bring your point up and forward fast, to *posta longa*, but hold the pass in reserve
3. As the defender reacts to the threat and comes to parry, dip your point out of the way, let his blade pass by, and bring your point back up
4. Pass in to strike.

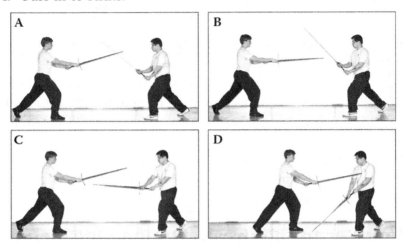

A Jan feints a thrust at Ken, who starts to parry; **B** Jan avoids Ken's parry; **C** As Ken's parry goes by, Jan picks up his point; **D** and passes in to strike.

If the defender sees this coming, he can of course parry it and strike—so at this stage it is a good idea to play a variation where the attacker will either feint, or counter with the pommel strike. The defender may counter the feint or the pommel strike, if he can.

Counter to the Break, Option Two: Parry and Pommel Strike

1. Start in *zenghiaro*, the defender waits in *porta di ferro*
2. Enter with a thrust, which the defender parries, driving your sword down
3. As he does so, yield and enter with the pommel strike.

A As Ken parries, Jan allows his point to be moved wide;
B and enters with a pommel strike.

Of course, as you do so, the defender can quite easily counter either with the simple pommel strike as before, or more interestingly, play a slight variation on the 14th play of the second master of *zogho largo* (in which the attacker lifts his hands to parry the *roverso* to the throat, and the defender enters. It works just as well as a counter to the pommel strike entry). So the drill would continue:

1. As your pommel strike comes in, the defender lifts his sword, redirecting yours away to his right;
2. He drops his hilt over your forearm and
3. Grabbing his blade by the point with his left hand
4. Smacks you in the face with his sword
5. And throws you to the ground.

For a more gentle approach, he can throw you forwards by placing his sword on the right side of your neck, or backwards by getting his blade past your head and pulling.

Counter to the Break, Option Three: Takedown

If the sword is irrecoverable (as in the case where the defender has stepped on it), my preferred continuation is an adaptation of one of the dagger plays, as Fiore does not address the issue directly himself.

1. Start in *zenghiaro*, the defender is in porta *di ferro*
2. Enter with a thrust, which the defender parries, driving your sword down, passing across to step on it
3. As the step lands, drop your trapped sword and pass in
4. Controlling the defender's sword arm with your right hand and
5. Find the defender's face with your left hand
6. Pass again behind the defender to throw, being careful of the sword.

NB: See the notes and exercises on pp. 19-27 of *The Medieval Dagger* for instruction on falling safely, and takedowns, before attempting this exercise!

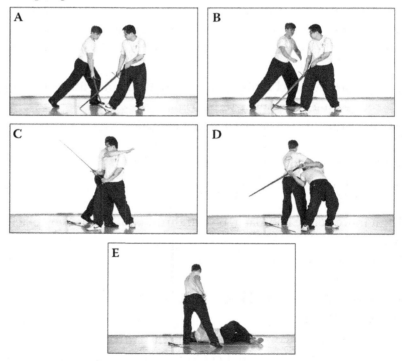

A Ken breaks Jan's thrust and steps on his sword; **B** Jan drops his sword and finds Ken's elbow; **C** And steps in; **D** and throws Ken; **E** maintaining control of Ken's sword throughout.

Tying Up Loose Ends:

So far we've seen the following remedies:

- Parry from the right against a cut
- Parry from the left against a cut
- Exchange the thrust from the right
- Break the thrust, from right and left side guards. And the counter-remedies have been:
- Yield and pommel strike
- Feint
- Parry his riposte
- Enter to wrestle (your sword has been taken away). And the counter-counter-remedies:
- Deflect the opponent's pommel strike and make your own pommel strike
- After you opponent's feint, parry again.

So what do you do if the opponent parries your riposte? Well, see under counter-remedies ... and what if he enters? Either hit him with your sword or beat him with your wrestling and dagger skills.

This begins to get very complicated. We can simplify things by starting on the left hand side, and further still by holding the sword in one hand. Here's how:

The Sword in One Hand

This is where Fiore begins the plays of sword against sword. The weapon is held in one hand, though there is no suggestion that it is anything other than a normal longsword (these actions are not specifically for a one-handed sword).

The Sword In One Hand Guard:

This position is held rear-weighted, with the right foot forwards.

The sword is hanging comfortably from the arm, with just enough tension in your grip to keep the point horizontal. I find it easiest to get into this position with a relaxed *mandritto fendente*, continuing the motion with a *volta stabile* to get the weight onto my back foot.

Ken stands in the guard of the master of the sword in one hand.

From here the instruction is to beat aside any attack. In practice, this is either a cut or a thrust. Against a cut, the parry is a blow coming up in the normal *sottano* line, accompanied by an *accrescere fora di strada*. Think "up", not forwards or back. As the sword arm rises allow the back arm to swing comfortably up and forwards. The end position is just like a *fenestra* held in one hand with the weight on the front foot.

Ken stands with the sword raised to a fenestra position.

When defending against a cut, one of three things will happen: you either beat aside the incoming sword, or the parry saves you but the sword is still threateningly in contact with yours, or the attack blows through. Leaving aside this last possibility, for which the only solution is *parry better*, let's have a look at what to do with these first two.

Attacker Cuts, Defender's Parry Beats It Aside

1. Wait in the guard of the master of sword in one hand
2. Attacker cuts
3. Parry with a vigorous, full *roverso sottano*, using your true edge, and supporting the motion with an *accrescere fora di strada* (right foot to the right)
4. The attacker's sword is beaten wide, so strike a *mandritto fendente*.

A Mikko attacks with a mandritto fendente; Ken parries; **B** Mikko's sword is beaten wide, Ken strikes. (Note that the blades first meet middle to middle; this photo was taken a moment later.)

There may be many reasons that the parry fails to beat the attacker's sword into next week. Perhaps the attack is better supported than the parry, or the attacker modifies his blow to bind the sword (more on this in the next chapter). Let's not worry about why just now, and focus on what.[14]

Attacker Cuts, Parry Sticks

1. Wait in the guard of the master of sword in one hand
2. Attacker cuts
3. Parry as before, with the *accrescere fora di strada* (right foot to the right)
4. Attacker resists the parry
5. Pass in with your left foot and reach with your left hand, keeping your sword hand high, and strike.

This may lead to just controlling the arm, or a full wrap, depending on what the attacker does and/ or how deeply you pass in.

A Mikko strikes, Ken parries, Mikko's sword does not go wide;
B so Ken enters, wraps Mikko's arms and thrusts.

---

14 I cracked this interpretation when a senior student was striking without undue force, but his less experienced partner just could not beat his sword wide. So I told him to enter instead. And suddenly I understood to the rationale behind these two plays.

Finally, let's deal with the thrust. From this position, all thrusts are handled the same way: break it to the ground, down and to the right.

1. Wait in the guard of the master of sword in one hand
2. Attacker thrusts
3. Beats the thrust down to the right with the *accrescere fora di strada* (right foot to the right)
4. Enter, controlling the attacker's elbow and, if you're feeling vicious
5. Pass behind to throw him or perhaps cut his throat.

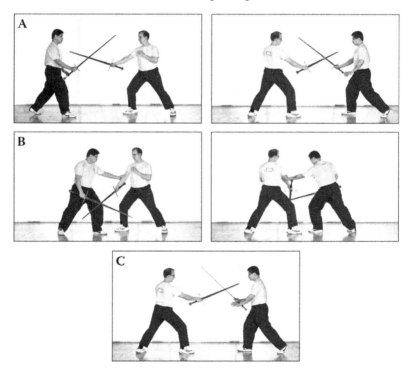

A Mikko attacks with a thrust; Ken parries, stepping offline;
B driving Mikko's sword down, and passing across finds Mikko's elbow.
C Ken's action can also be done with the false edge.

By choosing to wait in this guard, you have drastically reduced the possible permutations of the crossing that will happen when you parry. This is because you're starting on the left and by holding the sword in one hand, you can't fight a sticky cut—you have to yield.

What, then, is the fundamental difference between defence from the left and the right? At this stage, the primary difference is in the defender's footwork when dealing with an incoming cut, but mechanically, the defence from the right closes the line of the incoming attack and is then redirected to the target. This can be done in one fluid motion, curving your sword through *frontale* and striking immediately. When defending from the left, the attack must be beaten up and clear, as it must pass over your centre—this requires a more powerful blow, and given the mechanics of holding the sword, the follow-on strike (riposte) requires a 180 degree change of direction for the sword (up-down). Fiore explicitly refers to this difference in the text for the spear guard *mezana porta di ferro*.

Punishing the Opponent's Mistakes

We have by no means covered all of Fiore's sword plays, but from this point, you have at least a solid grounding in basic defensive and offensive tactics and techniques. I've put this next set of plays here in their own section because they depend on the attacker making a mistake: either over-committing to a strike, cutting to a low target and exposing his head, or something similar. These actions are found in many other systems, as under-trained fighters are a ubiquitous problem, and even a well-trained swordsman can make this kind of tactical error because these mistakes *work* if the opponent hasn't trained to counter them. They are very important to know, but as far as possible, I try to avoid having my students repeat sub-optimal actions in drill. There is a fundamental difference in doing something right but being countered, and making a mistake that your opponent exploits. If you don't see why these are mistakes, consider this: Fiore never shows them working, only being countered.

So, get these down, but remember when it's your turn to be the stooge, you're being punished for a mistake.

Let's take them in the order they appear in the treatise: the 5th to 8th plays of the second master of *zogho largo*.

The Peasant's Blow

Most treatises deal with the problem of the under-trained, over-committed attacker. Fiore calls him a *villano*, a peasant. Here he attacks with an unstoppably hard overhand blow (we will not dignify it with the term *mandritto fendente*). Fiore's instructions are extremely specific:

1. Await the peasant's blow in a narrow stance, left foot forwards (try *tutta porta di ferro* to start with)
2. When he comes to strike, meet his sword in the middle (i.e. parry with *frontale*)
3. Stepping out of the way with the front foot
4. And passing across
5. Letting his sword slide off to the ground and
6. Strike him
7. If he should pull back, and avoid your strike
8. Follow him and bind his sword from above
9. (then hit him, though Fiore doesn't mention it).

The most common error here is letting your point trail to the right when you parry, which exposes your head and your hands. Throw the point into a proper *frontale*, and then let the force of the peasant's blow drive it down and around, while you keep your hands high. Good grounding and a relaxed grip are essential.

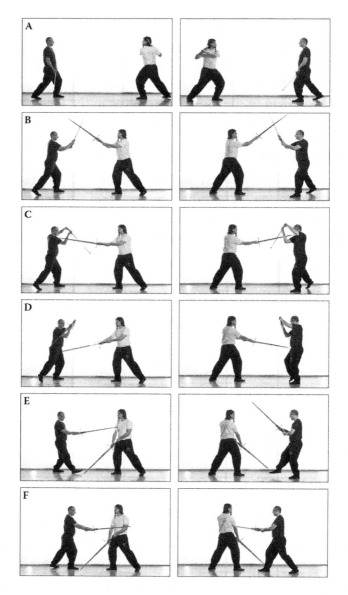

A Guy waits for Joni's attack; **B** As Joni strikes, Guy meets his sword, stepping offline; **C** Joni's blow pushes Guy's sword around; **D** Guy's sword comes free; **E** Guy strikes while passing and; **F** Guy's point arrives in Joni' chest.

Cutting the Leg

Fiore tells us that the only time you should cut to the leg is when one of you is on the ground.

Again, just about every fencing treatise punishes this mistake the same way—as he cuts for your leg, slip it back and hit him in the head, for offences against geometry.

Your sword is attached to your arm, which connects to the body at the shoulder. So the longest attack you can make is at a target at shoulder height. As you aim lower, the target must be closer to you for you to be able to hit it.

A At shoulder height, Guy reaches Ilpo;
B As Guy's point lowers, he can no longer reach.

This can occur either when your opponent attacks your leg in the first place, or after you parry his attack, he ripostes with a low blow. Or he may feint, and as you parry, cut low. By this stage in your practice, you really don't need me to write out everything as a drill, so go ahead and set up these versions of the play. As the 7th play of the second master of *zogho largo* (who shows us the middle crossing of the sword in wide play) the only interpretation of the attacker's actions that is strictly canonical is when he continues his attack after the parry, because it follows from the master's crossing as shown. Other ways of doing it are applications of the lesson of the play.

A Ilpo attacks, Guy parries; B Ilpo drops his point to strike Guy's leg;
C Guy slips his leg back and strikes Ilpo in the head.

Kicking the Nuts

It's my belief that every book on martial arts needs at least one kick to the nuts (I even squeezed one into my rapier book *The Duellist's Companion*), and Fiore does not disappoint. The circumstances are that the swords are crossed near the hilts, with the points high (so, quite far away). You can't leave the cross to strike, as his sword might hit you; you can't grab his blade, it's too far away (I cover grabbing the blade in the next chapter, "Binds, Malice and Deceit"). So you boot him in the nuts "so his cover will falter", and then hit him as you like. Note that if your opponent is female a well-executed kick to the groin is still pretty effective, or so I have been told.

How did we get into this position? Given that this is the 8th play of the second master of *zogho largo*, we may assume that a) the player attacked b) we parried initially at middle to middle; and c) he did not bind (or at least not successfully). This kind of cross actually happens quite often in freeplay. When it does, it is usually because the attacker's momentum takes him in closer than the defender expected, and the crossing slides from the middle down to the hilts. Strictly speaking, no-one has made a mistake here, but neither has either player executed a truly successful attack or parry, so this seemed the proper place to put this play.

A Ilpo attacks, Guy parries;
B the swords slide together;
C Guy kicks Ilpo in the nuts.

Amongst friends of course, the kick to the nuts should not make contact. In freeplay my students are expected to a) wear a groin guard; b) kick to the well-protected stomach; and c) if they drop their partner with a real kick in the nuts, their partner gets to say (when he gets his breath back) how many push-ups they'll do by way of atonement. I'll leave it up to you whether you want to practise this technique at all.

Fiore tells (but does not show) us how to counter: when the kick comes in, catch it with your left hand, and throw the kicker to the ground.

A As Guy kicks, Ilpo drops his left hand and sweeps Guy's foot off target; **B** sweeping it up to destabilize him; **C** and passes in to throw.

Chapter Nine

BINDS, MALICE, AND DECEIT

I n almost every sword fight, the blades will meet at some point. With the longsword, that is usually but not always as the attack is parried. The first meeting of the blades is in many respects the thing that defines what can follow, and who will win. Whoever masters the crossing, gets the strike. All medieval swordsmanship sources emphasise what happens when the blades cross. This crossing can be reduced to three critical factors: where on the blades the cross occurs, where the points of the swords end up, and how much pressure is being exerted. Up to now, almost every parry has been aimed middle to middle, and has worked as intended, beating the sword aside, with the exception of the "sticky" cut against the position of the sword in one hand. This was by way of introduction to the idea of binding the sword, which is a process of gaining mechanical control of your opponent's weapon using your own.

In combat, the crossings of the sword happen so fast, and ideally last for such a short time, that it is unusual to respond to their specific conditions *as they occur*; more commonly, cues in our opponent's prior movements indicate what will happen when the blades meet. It is nonetheless useful to analyse the possible cross-ings, to get an idea of what may occur and what you *should* do about it. This section is a bit like explaining traffic lights to a driving student.

Let's start with where on the blades the cross is made. Most of the time you would be aiming for a cross at the middle of both swords, but Fiore divides the blade (as we have seen) into three parts: the *tutta spada* (the first section near the hilt), the *mezza spada* (the middle section) and the *punta di spada* (the last section, near the point). Mathematicians will have no difficulty working out that there are nine possible combinations of places on the sword where the crossing happens:

You/Opponent	You/Opponent	You/Opponent
tutta/tutta	mezza/tutta	Punta/tutta
tutta/mezza	mezza/mezza	Punta/mezza
tutta/punta	mezza/punta	Punta/punta

We must also consider the position of your point, close enough to be a threat, or wide, and his, close or wide, so multiply 9x4 and we get 36 possible crossings. Add to that (or rather multiply) the degree of pressure between the blades (let's be binary and say strong or weak—we could have a dozen gradations of strength) and we have 72 crossings. And lastly, which side is open—inside, outside or neither? So multiply by three and we get 216 possible meetings of the swords. That is patently absurd. Let's carve it down a bit.

What matters most is what you can do from a given relationship of the blades. In practice, it is only possible to apply pressure when meeting at the *mezza* or the *tutta* of your sword. So where there is a *punta* involved, that sword (or both) are always weak in the bind.

Also, when crossed at the points, the points of the swords can't be threatening either of you directly, as you are either too far away, or they are pointing up or to the side, so it can always be considered "wide". Likewise, when crossed at the *tuttas*, the points must be wide, or there would have been a strike already, you're so close. Where one point is against another's *mezza* or *tutta*, there should be sufficient leverage advantage that the *punta* is always weak in the bind, and will be driven wide. So, that same table now looks like this:

You/Opponent	You/Opponent	You/Opponent
tutta/tutta: both points wide, bind is strong. Kick to nuts.	**mezza/tutta**: he is strong, you are weaker, cover and enter.	**punta/tutta**: he is much stronger, you are weak. Cover and enter
tutta/mezza: you are stronger. Bind his sword out of the way and strike.	**mezza/mezza**: points may be wide or close, pressure may be strong or weak. Many possible continuations.	**punta/mezza**: he is strong, you are weak. Cover and enter
tutta/punta: you are much stronger. Control his sword and strike (e.g. exchange thrusts).	**mezza/punta**: you are stronger, but his sword is close. Grab his tip and strike.	**punta/punta**: strike first on whichever side is open.

It should go without saying that you strike on the side he is open; if you aren't sure, if neither side is clearly open, go to the other side (so if your sword is on the right of his, go to the left). This is because whatever force he is using to keep you out of the centre should open that line when you release your counter-pressure.

The only part of the table where there is any real ambiguity is the middle one, where the swords have met in the middles: the points may be wide or close, and the bind may be strong or weak. If his point is close, and the bind is strong, you must enter into the close plays. This crossing leads only to the *zogho stretto*. If his point has been driven wide, and/or there is little pressure in the bind, it is safe to either grab his blade and strike (if it is close) or just strike (if his point is wide). These are examples of *zogho largo*.

Four Crossings Drill

At this stage, it is worthwhile setting up static crossings, having a look at them, and seeing why one technique or another makes sense from that point. Let's start with the most important set of four crossings:

1. Crossed at the middle, opponent's point driven wide, so strike to his arm and chest (second play second master *zogho largo*). You've done this before: see pp. 97–99
2. Crossed at the middle, opponent's point close enough to grab, no pressure in the bind, so grab and strike (third play second master *zogho largo*).[15]
3. Crossed at the middle, points in presence, pressure in the bind: opponent's open on the inside, so grab his sword handle (second play of *zogho stretto*).
4. Crossed at the middle, points in presence, pressure in the bind: opponent's open on the outside, so pommel strike (third play of *zogho stretto*).

Ken and Joni are crossed, middle to middle; Ken's point is wide. ...

---

15 Don't worry, grabbing the blade is quite safe, even with sharp swords and no gloves, and even more so with blunts. Just don't let it slide through your hand. I demonstrate this to the sceptical by taking a sharp longsword in a half-sword grip and thrusting it hard into a target: I have never been cut doing it.

... so Joni steps offline striking over the arm.

Ken's point is close enough to grab; ...

... so Joni steps offline left, grabbing Ken's sword and strikes.

Ken's point is close, and there is pressure in the bind ...

... so Joni binds Ken harder, enters, grabbing Ken's hilt.

Ken's point is close and he is binding Joni hard ...

... so Joni enters and pommel strikes.

It is critical to note here that it takes two to create a crossing. You may intend to beat his sword wide, but he may have other ideas.

Finding the Stretto

This drill builds on the counterattack we saw in Chapter Five. This is the beginning of "the Stretto Form of First Drill" in my syllabus.

1. You and the attacker are both ready in *posta di donna destra*
2. Attacker strikes with *mandritto fendente*, aiming at your head
3. Counterattack with a *mandritto fendente* half blow, aiming to meet the middle of the attacker's sword with the middle of your own, stepping diagonally right with your right foot (*passo fora di strada*).

Done right, this leads to the attacker having stopped with your point in his face. The attacker has no option but to redirect his blow to bind your sword:

4. As your sword approaches his, the attacker redirects to parry it, binding your point away from his face

At this point the swords are bound together, with neither player having a clear advantage. Of course, whoever sees it first will get their counter in first. The continuations looks like this:

5. Attacker reaches over with his left hand and grabs your hilt, and strikes
6. Or, you could immediately enter with a pommel strike.

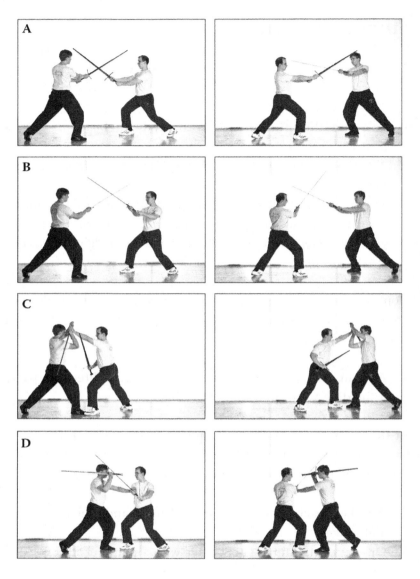

A Mikko has attacked; Jan counterattacks, passing out of the way;
B Mikko parries Jan's counterattack;
C Mikko enters, grabbing Jan's hilt.
D or Jan sees it first, and enters in with a pommel strike.

What makes this drill more challenging than the first version is that rather than each action following on from the previous action (defence follows attack, etc), the counter-remedy *prevents* the remedy; the counter-counter-remedy *prevents* the counter-remedy.[16] Strictly speaking, because the original remedy is never completed, it is doubtful whether Fiore would even use the terms counter-remedy, etc. Both of the plays (the hilt grab and the pommel strike) are possible continuations from the crossing at the middle of the sword in *zogho stretto*. It is clear (and Fiore explicitly states) that when the *stretto* crossing occurs, either party can act. Indeed, in the Getty one wears the crown, and the other the garter; in the Pisani-Dossi, they are both crowned. This drill lends itself to all sorts of advanced variations, which can be found on the Wiki, and will form a large part of the next book in this series.

Common variations to watch for include:

- The attacker parrying the counterattack so strongly that his point goes too wide; the defender should strike on the other side with a *roverso fendente*. This is effectively an application of the lesson of the *colpo di villano* play (see p. 153).
- The attacker collecting the counterattack so well that he can immediately strike with a thrust; this takes you into Exchange of Thrusts territory.
- The defender grabbing the tip of the attacker's sword as he parries and doing the 12th play of the *zogho stretto* (this is described in detail below).

Now let's play this same game of binding the defender's action, with the defender starting on the left, and note that it works a little differently. This is the "Stretto Form of Second Drill".

---

16 In modern fencing terms, the counter-attack is parried with an action in counter-time; the action in counter-time is foiled by a feint in time (in which the counter-attack is done to draw the parry).

1. Wait in *zenghiaro* (so, right foot forwards), attacker starts in *posta di donna destra*
2. Attacker strikes with a *mandritto fendente*
3. You parry by beating the incoming sword up and to the right, as before. Remember the *accrescimento fora di strada* (step out of the way with your front (right) foot)
4. Attacker binds the parry (**A**), directing his sword to the right. If successful, this allows him to then cut at your head (**B**), or enter in (**C**)
5. You immediately pass in, using your left arm to envelop both the attacker's arms (**D**)
6. Presenting your point to the attacker's face.

Note that the attacker's bind takes his point *away* from your face, making your *accrescere* doubly useful to you, as it neatly sets up your continuation.

A Guy has attacked, Mikko parried, Guy bound Mikko's sword to the right; **B** creating an opportunity to strike …

C or enter; **D** as Guy binds, Mikko enters.

Note that this is almost exactly what happened when you defended from the guard of the sword in one hand, and the attack was "sticky".

If we compare this to the same situation where you parried from the right, an *accrescere* would not have had the same effect—indeed, it would probably make the situation worse as the attacker's bind might immediately stab you in the face. This to my mind is the fundamental guiding principle behind the defender's choice to start on the left or on the right. Starting on the left commits you to a bigger, more obvious parry, but reduces the number of possible variations on the crossing you would have to deal with. All you need to worry about is whether the attack is beaten wide or not. Starting on the right allows for a much larger range of more closely tailored (and therefore efficient) defences, but requires you to be able to make correct decisions very fast under a lot of pressure. Any wonder then that Fiore begins and ends the plays of the sword with a defence from the left?

Fiore actually gives us a couple of plays in the *zogho stretto* (the 11th and 12th) that specifically deal with defenders covering from one side or another. They are too useful to overlook. The critical factor as I see it is to remember that these plays follow on from a *stretto* crossing, so the parry has clearly not beaten the attack wide.

Against an opponent covering from the left:

1. You are in *posta di donna destra*, partner in *zenghiaro* (or any left side guard)
2. Attack with a *mandritto fendente*
3. As partner parries, bind his sword and
4. Grab his pommel with your left hand, throwing his sword over his left shoulder, and thrust underneath.

Against an opponent covering from the right:

1. You are in *posta di donna destra*, partner in *tutta porta di ferro* (or any right side guard)
2. Attack *mandritto fendente*
3. As partner counterattacks, bind his sword and
4. Grab his sword tip with your left hand, and hit him in the face (mask) with his own weapon.

One of the more persistent beginners' mistakes when attacking is to aim for the defender's sword rather than his head (or other target). Done by accident, this just messes up everyone's technique. However, it is perfectly correct and often advisable to deliberately draw the defender's action and prevent him from completing it by redirecting your sword to bind his. Done deliberately for good reason, this can create the first play of the first master of the *zogho largo*, thus:

First Master of the *Zogho Largo* Drill:

1. Attacker ready in *posta di donna destra*. You wait in *tutta porta di ferro*
2. Attacker enters with a *mandritto fendente*, aiming at your head
3. Parry with *frontale*
4. Attacker redirects the *fendente* before contact towards his own *frontale* position, so the swords meet near the points
5. At this stage either player can strike: whoever recognises the nature of the crossing first will doubtless win. This is probably why both swordsmen are crowned in the Pisani-Dossi version of this play. For the sake of sticking with the general pattern of the treatise though, let's have you (the defender) be master of the crossing
6. The attacker's bind opens his outside line, so take your point up and over the attacker's and strike down on the other side.

A Jan (on left) has parried Auri's attack; Auri has redirected her blow to meet Jan's sword, moving it aside a little. **B** Auri strikes on the same side. **C** or if Jan sees it first, he can strike on the other side.

It is of course also possible that the attacker is deliberately feinting to draw the parry to bind it, and will strike on the same side if he manages to open the line, or on the other side if not.

Feints

With so much riding on what happens when the swords cross, there is a strong temptation to avoid crossing altogether. When you persuade your opponent that you will attack one target, and as he closes that line, you strike him in the opening line that his movement creates, the first action is called a feint.

Fiore does not discuss the feints explicitly (though guards such as *fenestra*, *longa* and *bicorno* are "deceitful", and we have the aforementioned *punta falsa,* to be covered in Volume Three), but Vadi does in chapter 12 of *De Arte Gladiatoria Dimicandi*:

Feints call out to obfuscate
They hide from the other's defence. Do not let him understand,
What you want to do from one side or the other.
(Translation mine, from *Veni VADI Vici*)

You have already seen one feint as a counter to the breaking of the thrust on pp. 143–44. The rules of feinting are pretty simple: you must create a credible threat. As your opponent responds, your strike should take less time than his second parry. Your end position should also close the line of his riposte. He may not notice that his parry has failed, and may hit you as you hit him. That he has made a mistake doesn't make his blow any less effective.

In practice, you can feint high, strike low; feint low, strike high; feint right, strike left; and feint left, strike right. You may feint with a cut to land a thrust, feint with a cut to land a cut, feint with a thrust to land a cut, and feint with a thrust to land a thrust. Just whatever you do, make sure your sword is in the way of his when your strike lands.

My favourite feinting drill exploits the nature of the guard *bicorno* to draw a panicky parry, and effortlessly strike on the other side:

1. Begin in *posta di donna destra*, rear-weighted
2. Partner is in any guard, right or left side (*zenghiaro* is illustrated)
3. Snap into *bicorno*, with a *volta stabile*. If your partner hasn't moved, you should be able to hit him before he can parry, so a credible threat has been created
4. Partner begins his parry during your *volta stabile*
5. As you reach *bicorno* at the end of your *volta stabile*, dip your point under his parry and up the other side
6. Then walk your thrust in, striking his mask (gently), keeping your sword between his weapon and you. Have your partner riposte anyway to make sure you are covered: if he hits you, you made a mistake!

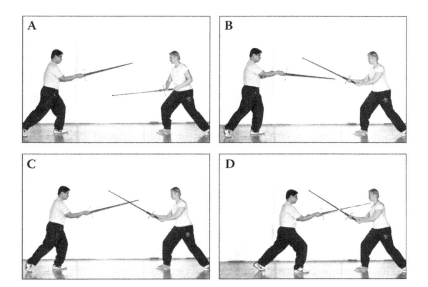

A Ken's feint is drawing Auri's parry from her left; **B** Ken dips his point to avoid it; **C** bringing it up on the other side; **D** and passes to strike.

The counter to this action is of course a second parry; as your feint comes up the other side of his sword, your partner can parry it. Feints rely on *selling* the blow, so your partner believes that it is the real attack. More on this in the freeplay chapter.

Hierarchy of Defence

Let us look at the basic hierarchy of fencing actions. We have seen attacks, parries, counterattacks, binds, and feints; a simple guide to what counters what might be helpful. In short:

Who moves first? One or other player must move first, or both move simultaneously. Leaving aside any pre-combat manoeuvres, when entering into measure to strike, there should be a clear threat made. This can be met with a parry, or a counterattack (let's leave out running away).

Assuming the parry is successful, it is normally followed by a riposte. The parry can be countered by a) a feint, which avoids it to strike on the other side, or b) an angulation, which goes around it on the same side, or c) the attacker can parry the riposte or counterattack into it.

The counterattack can be made with opposition (closing the line of the attack as in the exchange of thrusts) or with avoidance (such as stepping out of the way and sniping at the hands). In either case, it should be parried.

So, how do we perform and counter an angulated attack, and a counterattack to the hands?

The Angulated Attack

There are two ways to angulate an attack: either move offline when striking so the attack goes in a straight line to the target, but at an unexpected angle and so gets past the parry; or as your opponent parries, change the angle of your sword to reach around it. Fiore describes the former in the play of the pollax in *posta di donna* versus *dente di zenghiaro*; he does not describe the latter. But it is a useful thing to know, so:

1. Begin in *donna destra*, the defender waits in *tutta porta di ferro*
2. Attack with a *mandritto fendente*
3. Defender comes to parry with *frontale*
4. As your strike meets his parry, turn your hands over, angle a thrust around his sword
5. Enter with the left hand controlling his arm.

A Guy has attacked, Auri parries;

B Guy angulates, passing in and checking Auri's sword arm with his left hand.

Countering this action is perhaps best done with the third play of the second master of *zogho largo,* in which the defender grabs the blade:

1. Attacker in *donna destra,* you wait in *tutta porta di ferro*
2. Partner attacks with a *mandritto fendente*
3. Parry with *frontale*; as the blades meet his point remains close, so grab it
4. And strike.

A Auri spots the nature of the crossing in time, and grabs Guy's blade;

B and strikes.

Fiore also shows a variation where after grabbing your opponent's blade, you hit him while stamping on his knee. Don't do this until you've been trained to kick accurately and consistently, or you might break your partner's leg. As kicks form such a small part of Fiore's repertoire, and would require a chapter of their own to cover in sufficient detail, I have largely left them out of this book, but you can find our basic kicking curriculum on the Syllabus Wiki.

The Counterattack to the Hands:

This action bedevils a lot of modern longsword play, and doesn't appear much in our medieval sources. I think this is due to two main things: a well-executed attack doesn't leave the hands open to it, and at speed with sharps, it is too risky with these weapons as it does not necessarily cripple the attacker (especially considering the thickness of medieval clothing), and it provides no structural defence against his blow.

With that in mind, let us set this up as the attacker deliberately drawing this action to counter it. Again for simplicity's sake, we will stick with our usual set-up. I recommend wearing gauntlets for this so the defender can relax a bit and make contact with your hands if you make a mistake.

1. Begin in *donna destra*, defender waits in *tutta porta di ferro* or *donna destra*
2. Attack with a *mandritto fendente*, letting your sword-point trail slightly behind, opening a line to your hands
3. Defender slices down with a *fendente* to the back of your left hand, stepping away
4. Turn your blade into his attack to close the line, and redirect your attack as a thrust to the face.

A Auri has attacked; Mikko counterattacks to the hands;
B Auri parries Mikko's cut; **C** and enters to thrust.

Cool Tricks

Fiore ends the plays of *zogho stretto* with a set of disarms—perhaps the most witheringly humiliating way to end a fight. Two and a half years after I founded my school, my top student at the time succeeded in disarming me in freeplay. It remains one of the highlights of my teaching career, as it meant that I had succeeded in training someone from scratch, in pretty quick time, to be able to pull off a cool trick on a much more experienced opponent.

Fiore shows us four versions—I'll take you through the first, as it's my favourite. This can be arrived at in at least three ways:

- The defender covers from the left (i.e. *zenghiaro*), beating the incoming sword away.
- The defender covers from the right; the attacker enters with the disarm.
- The defender counterattacks from the right, the attacker parries; the defender enters with the disarm.

As the last version fits exactly with the Getty manuscript, let's opt for that one.

1. Wait in *tutta porta di ferro* or *posta di donna*
2. Attacker strikes a *mandritto fendente*
3. Counterattack, passing out of the way
4. Attacker parries your blow, creating the bind
5. Turn your sword to find the flat of the attacker's blade with your handle
6. Reach over the attacker's arms with his left, passing across with the left foot
7. Wrapping his arms, execute a *tutta volta*, passing your right foot behind you
8. Use the leverage on the sword and the momentum of the turn to strip the sword out of the attacker's hands.

A having his counterattack parried, Guy enters on the outside;

B wrapping Mikko's arms with his left and bearing down on his blade;

C stripping the weapon from Mikko's hands with a tutta volta.

This is the *soprano tor di spada*, the disarm from above. If the attacker's hands were too high to reach over, grab his pommel instead (the *sottano tor di spada*, disarm from below). If his hands are in the middle, grab his hilt while torqueing his sword around with the same handle-to-flat arrangement (the *mezano tor di spada*).

A Guy grabs Mikko's hilt between his hands;

B Guy grabs Mikko's pommel.

Note that in all the above plays, the opponent's sword is being turned in a big clockwise circle, using your left hand as the centre, and the contact between the handle of your sword and the opponent's flat as the main point where force is exerted. Make sure you get his flat, and keep the point of contact reasonably far from his hilt for leverage. In class I often have students practise the motion out of context. Have your partner stand in *posta longa*, grab his blade with your right hand and wrap over his arms with your left, making the turn in the plane of his flat. Then try it using your sword handle in place of your right hand. Then put it back into its context. If the wrap makes it a bit tricky, then try grabbing the pommel and the blade to make the turn. If you did that from the *stretto* crossing, first grabbing his blade with your right hand, then dropping your sword to grab his pommel with your left hand, then making the turn, you would be doing the last, 23rd, play of the *zogho stretto.*

This concludes the basic technical material of the book. Well done for getting this far! From here on we will look at ways of making the potentially bewildering array of options available to you under changing conditions.

Chapter Ten

PREPARING FOR FREEPLAY

The technical drills so far should give you an idea of how the system fits together and how the techniques themselves can often be matched against each other. Let's take just one, the breaking of the thrust, countered with a pommel strike, countered with a takedown, and see just how many decisions were made between the facing off and the final action:

1. Defender chose to start on the right
2. Attacker chose to attack with a thrust
3. Attacker chose to thrust from the left
4. Defender chose to break the thrust (so identified the attack correctly)
5. Attacker chose to yield to the parry and enter
6. Defender parried the pommel strike and went for the takedown
7. Attacker failed to counter the takedown.

That is a simply staggering list of decisions. If we limited each option to only two, we get a ridiculous decision tree, with a total of 2x2x2x2x2x2x2=256 possible finishes. But there are many more options (e.g. the attacker could have chosen to bind, angulate, feint, etc etc). So how is it possible to learn this art? Simply put, of that 256, about 100 would finish on a pommel strike, about 100 with a grip of some kind (such as our middle lock), about 50 with a simple cut or thrust, and the rest would be divided up amongst a few cool tricks. So what you need now is a means to hold the whole system in memory, to be able to practise finding the right technique spontaneously.

I have organised the longsword syllabus for my school as a set of basic drills to be memorised, and a set of multipliers which when applied to the set drills create the entire system, every play, every concept, in a reproducible and repeatable way.

The Four Set Drills:

First Drill: Cover from the Right. (http://www.swordschool.com/wiki/index.php/First_drill) This starts with the defender in *tutta porta di ferro*, and the attacker in *posta di donna destra*, because these are the first two guards shown in the section of the 12 guards.

The attack is *mandritto fendente*, defender parries with *frontale* and steps offline to strike over the arm; attacker yields to parry and enters with pommel strike; defender counters with his own pommel strike.

Second Drill: Cover from the Left. (http://www.swordschool. com/wiki/index.php/Second_drill) This starts with the defender in dente *di zenghiaro*, because this is the start of the last play of the sword out of armour. The attacker is in *posta di donna destra*. The attack is *mandritto fendente*, defender parries with the *accrescere* and strikes to the head; attacker yields to the parry and enters with a *ligadura mezana* wrap and pommel strike; defender counters with the *ligadura sottana*. This is an explicit reference to the sections of the sword in one hand and the dagger.

Exchange of Thrust: (http://www.swordschool.com/wiki/index.php/Exchange_of_thrust) both attacker and defender in *tutta porta di ferro*.

Breaking the Thrust: (http://www.swordschool.com/wiki/index.php/Breaking_the_thrust) attacker in *dente di zenghiaro*, defender in *tutta porta di ferro*.

As a pair, these thrusting plays refer explicitly to the spear section. These four drills form the base.

Four Corners Drill

The first multiplier is called the "four corners drill", and is hinted at in the set-up for the base four. First, with the defender remaining in *tutta porta di ferro*, the attacker changes the guard of origin and therefore usually the line of his attack, from his right shoulder, to his left, then his left hip, then his right hip. Note that these last two are the set-up for the break and the exchange respectively. The attacker may choose any guards he knows that start from these points (both *donna* and *fenestra* are coded for by "shoulder" for instance), and may cut or thrust as he likes.

Then the defender starts from each "corner" in turn while the attack remains constant (*mandritto fendente* from *posta di donna*). If you expand this to include the centreline guards (*mezana porta di ferro, breve, longa*), you get a total of 144 combinations! This is bound to throw up problem areas, such as "how do I defend from *donna sinestra* against a *mandritto fendente*?". You might have noticed that you can look on Second Drill as a variation of First Drill, using the four corners multiplier. It starts with the same attack, but a different starting guard for the defender.

All of this material can be "stored" in Part One of the Cutting Drill, which as you probably know by now goes like so:

1. Begin in *posta di donna destra*
2. Cut a full *mandritto fendente* through *posta longa* to *dente di zenghiaro*, passing;
3. Cut a *roverso sottano* to *posta longa*, with the false edge, passing;
4. Go to *posta di donna destra*;
5. Cut a half mandritto fendente to *posta longa*;
6. Go to *posta di donna sinestra*;
7. Cut a full roverso fendente to *tutta porta di ferro*;
8. Cut a *mandritto sottano* to *posta longa*, false edge, passing;
9. Go to *donna sinestra*;
10. Cut a half *roverso fendente* to *posta longa*, passing;

11. Go to *donna destra.*

All four corners are represented, and any one of the blows may be executed as a thrust.

The Four Crossings Drill, and the Seven Crossings Drill

The second multiplier is the four crossings drill.

1. Crossed at the middle, partner's point driven wide, so strike to his arm and chest (second play second master *zogho largo*)
2. Crossed at the middle, partner's point close enough to grab, no pressure in the bind, so grab and strike (third play second master *zogho largo*)
3. Crossed at the middle, points in presence, pressure in the bind: he's open on the inside, so grab his sword handle (second play of *zogho stretto*)
4. Crossed at the middle, points in presence, pressure in the bind: he's open on the outside so pommel strike (third play of *zogho stretto*).

In their basic form, each of the four drills can be thought of as an example of the first of the four crossings—the attack is successfully beaten wide. So, how can each be varied to include the second, third or fourth of these crossings? For example, if we think of (2) as "point stays close but no pressure in the bind" it might stand in for a feint; used against the breaking of the thrust, for instance, and we have found another of the set drills that make up this book. Once the four crossings are understood, we expand it to seven:

1. Crossed at the middle, partner's point driven wide, so strike to his arm and chest (second play second master *zogho largo*)
2. Crossed at the middle, partner's point close enough to grab, no pressure in the bind, so grab and strike (third play second

master *zogho largo*)

3. Crossed at the middle, points in presence, pressure in the bind: he's open on the inside, so grab his sword handle (second play of *zogho stretto*)

4. Crossed at the middle, points in presence, pressure in the bind: you're stuck in the middle, so smash his hands up with your crossguard, and wrap with your left hand (eighth play of *zogho stretto*)

5. Crossed at the middle, points in presence, pressure in the bind: he's open on the outside so pommel strike (third play of *zogho stretto*)

6. Crossed at the middle, points in presence, a bit more pressure in the bind: it feels safe, so grab his blade and hit him with it (twelfth play of *zogho stretto*)

7. Crossed at the middle, there's so much pressure in the bind that his sword is moving away from you, so yield and strike on the other side (fifth play second master *zogho largo, colpo di villano*).

You could add to these what happens if the blades cross at the tips (first and second plays of the first master of *zogho largo*), what happens if you end up crossed at the *tutta spadas* (kick to the nuts, 8th play of the second master of the *zogho largo*), what happens if you end up with his point against your *tutta spada*, what happens when you are crossing from the left, etc. As a rule of thumb, avoid putting more than seven things in any drill, so if you want a complete catalogue of crossings and their solutions, I'd advise breaking them into groups of no more than seven.

Who Moves First?

The third multiplier we have already seen from the dagger plays in *The Medieval Dagger*: who moves first? In any set drill, you can a) start the drill with both players standing still in guard (this is the usual set-up for beginners to start with, and it's how I've written up all of the drills in this book); b) change who attacks; or c) draw the attack by some prior movement or invitation. In my salle we spend a lot of time doing basic drills, but starting from way out of measure. The trick is to arrive at the right time, in the right place, to do the initial actions of a particular drill, without exposing yourself. Refer to Pell work in Chapter Six for preparatory exercises for this.

In addition to these three multipliers we can add an action at the beginning or end of any drill, and drill any set of actions sequentially.

Add a Step

Another simple means to make a drill more useful is to allow the "loser" to counter the last step if he can. So for instance, you set up the breaking of the thrust drill, and, as the attacker counters, the defender may, if he sees it coming and can think up something useful to do, counter the attacker's action. There is in theory no end to this drill, as every action can be countered. Add one step at a time, and stop when it becomes difficult to remember how you got to where you are. This uses a set drill to set up a kind of slow freeplay.

Sequential Drilling

In this exercise, we go through all the likely options from a given starting point. That point might be *posta di donna* versus *dente di zenghiaro*, with a specified attacker (could be either one) and a specified attack (e.g. *mandritto fendente*). From this set-up, the possible actions include:

- Attack lands (parry fails)
- Parry is successful, defender strikes
- Parry is bound, attacker strikes
- Parry is successful, attacker yields and enters
- Parry is bound, defender yields and enters

- Parry is deceived (attacker feints), attacker strikes
- Parry is deceived, defender parries again and strikes.

Note that we have not yet gone beyond the counter-counter-remedy stage. To start with, these actions are trained in order; the attacker chooses one path or the other. The defender knows in which order the attacker's choices will be, and so should be able to make the counter-counter-remedy.

Degrees of Freedom

This is the beginning of the bridge between set basic drills and advanced fencing skill. At any stage in any drill, a set of decisions have been made. Systematically allowing a different choice to be made by one player, on the fly, introduces an element of unpredictability for the other player. For example, in the above drill we might allow the attacker to choose his counter-remedy at random. This can be either to develop the attacker's decision-making skills (so the defender is helping him), or to develop the defender's ability to adapt (so the attacker is helping him). When there is a choice like that to be made, we say there is a degree of freedom—the attacker in this case has one degree of freedom—one point in the drill where he gets to make a choice. The other has to respond appropriately in real time.

The "Rule of Cs"

The "Rule of Cs" is then applied to all of the above, in which every drill is first worked through with the players:

Co-operating in creating correct choreography.

Once that is easy, increase the difficulty by increasing intensity, or introducing a degree of freedom (e.g. is the attack a cut or thrust?), with one player adjusting the difficulty for the other to learn at their most efficient rate—if it works all the time, ramp it up—if it fails more than twice in ten reps, ease off a bit.

This is called:

Coaching correct actions.

Finally, the players each try within reason to make the drill work for them. In First Drill for instance, the degree of freedom that has just been coached might be that the attacker is either continuing with a pommel strike, or angulating around the parry. When coaching, he tries to make sure the defender can usually counter him; when competing, he just tries to make his action work. This can be dangerous if it gets out of hand, so be careful, and wear full protection just in case. In practice, the more experienced fencer should get most of the hits, without departing from the drill. This is fine, and gives a good indication of whether your training regime is working. So,

Compete.

There is a significant risk of this getting out of hand; be mindful as you play the drill competitively that you must stick to the constraints of the drill that you have both agreed on. Otherwise you lose track of the rationale behind what you are doing, and mistakes creep in that are difficult to spot and to trace back to their source.

To recap then, we have the following means of expanding on set drills:

- The four corners drill
- The four and seven crossings drills
- Sequential drilling
- Who moves first?
- Extending the drill

- Adding degrees of freedom—so either partner gets one or more decision points.
- The Rule of Cs

What we need now then is a drill that allows either person to attack or defend, with any action, and the play to continue until a technique is successfully concluded. We call it freeplay! But first, a short tactical summary.

Tactical Summary

When attacking, it doesn't much matter if you kill your opponent with a cut or a thrust. Arguably, the thrust arrives first, but the cut frees itself more easily, and does more immediate structural damage. If well-placed though, both finish the fight. So the primary tactical distinctions between cut and thrust concern what happens when the opponent parries (or tries to).

When cutting, we can divide the possible outcomes into six types, listed here in order of when during the strike they may occur:

1. Strike—the parry fails
2. Avoid the parry (i.e. feint)
3. Stopped—the parry stops the attack but does not open the line. Angulate
4. Anticipate cross, redirect the contact towards his point, and turn to the other side with your point (first play of first master zogho largo)
5. Yield to the parry (i.e. the parry is successful, but you enter immediately on the other side, for example with a pommel strike)
6. Allow the parry, then deal with his counter

When thrusting, there are fewer possibilities:

1. Avoid the parry (i.e. feint)
2. Strike—the parry fails
3. Yield to the parry (i.e. the parry is successful, but you turn immediately to the other side)
4. Allow the parry, then deal with his counter.

Thrusts are in general harder to see, and easier to redirect (by either attacker or defender). They are also much more effective against an armoured target—they can go through a light gambeson (which cuts will generally not), and are the blow of choice for getting through the gaps in armour (armpit, groin, visor etc.). Something to think about when you practise, and especially when going through the cutting drills alone.

Chapter Eleven

FREEPLAY!

The most fun you can have with your clothes on, and, done right, a superb learning environment. Please refer to the introduction, where I discuss the difference between freeplay versus combat, before getting your kit on and fencing your friends. Whatever your training goals, you should find the following guidelines for freeplay useful.

The President

Every bout should be presided, in that a senior scholar of the Art acts as a marshal. The role of the president is simply this—to ensure that the fencers finishing the bout are better than the ones who started it. This means a) no injuries b) both fencers are challenged to improve. There are many tricks the president may use to accomplish this, the most common of which I outline below.

There is also the matter of conditioned responses. If your goal is simply to excel in friendly freeplay, then stopping every time you get hit to acknowledge the blow is no bad thing. If however you wish to compete, or indeed to train for actual combat, then stopping when you think you've been hit is disastrous. Ideally, combatants in both arenas should train to stop only when a person in authority orders them to, or when the encounter is resolved to their own satisfaction. So part of the president's job is to create an environment where the combatants should continue until ordered to stop.

In my salle, the person presiding the bout is invested with almost unlimited authority. They can stop the bout at any time for any reason, impose fair or unfair conditions on the fencers, impose penalties for bad fencing (the usual one for a double hit is 10 push-ups each, done immediately before the match resumes), and all is forgiven him if both fencers finish the bout better than they started it.

Ideally, the president should have an excellent, trained fencing memory, and be able therefore to determine exactly what happened before, during, and after each hit. More on training your fencing memory below.

Constructing the Bout

In the judicial duel, the challenger may be obliged to open the fight with a committed attack. This means that as a swordsman you should be excellent at both defence and attack, as you cannot know which side you will take in future encounters. To replicate this, we often fence in rounds of three passes. In the first pass, the junior student attacks, the more senior defends. In the second, the senior attacks. In the third, either one can attack or defend as they like. If during the first or second pass the actions are inconclusive, the fencers usually keep going until a hit is scored. You can begin with the fencers in measure to strike with a pass, or, more commonly in my salle, the fencers begin far apart, and the one attacking (or both) are expected to approach in a vigorous and martial manner. This introduces an interesting layer of complexity.

Tippy-Tappy Sh!t

There is a tendency, when the attacker is not predetermined, or when the first attack is inconclusive either way, for what we call "tippy tappy sh!t" to develop: uncommitted flicks to no good effect. This calls for a halt and a reset. Likewise, when required to attack, it is necessary that the attacker does not shuffle about. If the fencers start in guard and in measure to strike with a pass, then the attacker must strike from the guard he is in, no adjustments. One useful way to break bad habits is to have the fencers choose their guards, knowing who will attack and who defend, and before saying "Fence", order them to keep the same guards but change who attacks. This encourages students to use guards differently, and to choose guards from which they can both attack and defend.

Fiore is explicit, in the final pages of the Pisani-Dossi manuscript, that the most important quality a fighter should possess is *audatia*: be audacious! When helping out at the student's freeplay session at the 2007 Western Martial Arts Workshop, I had two fencers under my eye, one much more experienced than the other. They were fencing with shinai-based swordlike objects, and kept getting double hits (both fencers tapped each other, as neither was treating the weapons as real).

My solution was to make the senior remove his padded jacket and fence in his mask, gloves and t- shirt (yes, he was also wearing trousers). Immediately, he started to be concerned about getting hit, and pulled off two or three lovely Fiore plays in succession, safely and in good form. Fear is a necessary part of freeplay, or how can you practise boldness?

Rewind and Replay

After every hit, it can be extremely useful to replay the actions that lead to it. If it occurs late in an exchange of blows, just the final three or four actions are necessary. Then the one who was hit gets to counter the action, by either preventing the mistake that lead to it, or by countering the final strike. For example:

- A attacks *mandritto fendente;* B parries from *zenghiaro;* A binds the parry and strikes.
- Replay it once, slowly. B realises what he should have done (enter). They then replay the hit slowly, and B enters as he should have done.
- At some point later in the bout, if A is a helpful soul, he will try the same hit again—B should notice it, and counter. Even if he fails B still knows what he has to practise.

Most fencers start with zero memory for the phrases of a bout. This makes it very inefficient to learn from freeplay—if you don't know what happened, how do you change it? If you find yourself unable to recall the phrase, then leave pure freeplay alone for a bit and work on your memory. This drill works best with three fencers, an attacker, a defender and an observer. Switch roles after each phrase, to develop your ability to remember phrases you have both done and seen.

- Designate an attacker and a defender.
- Allow free choice of attack and defence, but no continuations (attacker can't counter).
- Attacker attacks as he likes, defender tries to defend. Notice who gets hit.
- First one, then the other, describes in clear fencing language, in detail exactly what occurred.

For example: "Mary was in *coda longa*, I was in *posta di donna*. Mary attacked with a thrust to my face. I tried to exchange the thrust, but my sword caught on the back of my mask and I missed my parry. Mary's thrust landed in my face". Then Mary describes what she thought happened "well, I started in *tutta porta di ferro*, and attacked with a *mandritto fendente* ... (you'll be amazed how rarely you'll agree with each other to start with). Lastly, the observer states what he thought happened. If the observer doesn't have a reliable fencing memory, use a video camera too.

When one attack and one defence can be reliably described and repeated, add the attacker's counter. When that is easily recalled, then the defender can counter that, and so on. Once you have built it up so that you can accurately reproduce a phrase of at least six actions (three from each side), your memory is ready for useful freeplay.

Right and Wrong

If something is working in freeplay that you know is counter to the historical style, you have to ask yourself if your goal is to win matches in your freeplay context, or to replicate Fiore's art? If the former, keep doing it. If the latter, either change the rules of the bout so that the action fails, or be content to identify a gap between freeplay and the duel, and avoid doing the action even though it might "work".

If a technique from Fiore is not working in freeplay, the same questions apply. It is possible that the interpretation is wrong (so it isn't actually Fiore's technique), but assuming that the play is correct, then you are either doing it at the wrong time, or in the wrong context. For example, when your opponent thrusts, you try to exchange it, but it is always failing. Is the thrust committed enough? Are you executing the action correctly? Is the attacker behaving as he should, given that the weapons are supposed to be sharp?

One very common problem is being hit on the hands when attacking. This has two components:

• The initial attack
• The counterattack to the hands.

If your attack is executed incorrectly, your hands may be exposed—so the problem could be your technique. If your technique is reasonably good, then the defender is making a mistake by failing to deal with the threat presented, so you should be striking him.

We know that Fiore only shows us blows to the arms, not the hands, and then only *after* a parry, or as a redirection of the original attack. So the defender is acting outside the art. What can be done to take away his incentive to do so? You could just say "no hits to the hands count" but that has its own problems, like encouraging badly executed attacks. Better to make the attacker land his blow despite the hit to the hand, which is what would probably happen in combat: the blow to the hand is unlikely to stop the attack, it has to actually control the sword arm or remove the hand from the wrist to do so. You might also teach the attacker to draw the defender's hit to the hand and counter it.

So How to Fence?

Once you are sword in hand, standing in front of your opponent, there are basically two approaches to actually overcoming him.

Option one: close off his every avenue, crush his game, and spend your time looking for ways to hit him. Analyse his positions, his movements, identify his goals and thwart them. See his weaknesses and exploit them.

Option two: you can simply relax and let training take over, and hit him.

Of course, as you hit him either way, there is nothing much to choose between these approaches in terms of winning matches, but it is interesting to notice the different mindsets required in each case. In the former you focus on your opponent—everything you do is about denying him options. In the latter, you focus on yourself—everything you do is about staying comfortable. Whatever you do, stay in balance, in tune, relaxed, mobile. Don't get hit because it's not nice. Hit him because it's fun. At its best, this approach makes you feel like your opponent is running himself into your sword, striking into lines that are already closed, co-operating with his defeat. In short, bliss.

In my experience, most fencers focus on their opponent, and adapt their actions accordingly. I prefer to just do what I want, stay comfortable, and (more often than not) strike. The root difference is where your attention is placed—on the opponent, or yourself. If you are paying attention to your opponent, you are easily deceived. But if your attention is entirely on yourself, you won't notice what he does. The idea is to keep your primary focus on your sense of flow, and let your peripheral vision and general awareness keep track of your opponent. Experiment with both, and do the one that works for you.

Aesthetics and Learning Paradigms

One of the main differences between historical swordsmanship and other combat arts, is that it is not enough to do an action mechanically efficiently. To be accurate, the action must also be aesthetically correct. In other words, winning is not enough—we have to win in the correct style, or what we are doing ceases to be historical. This is not such an issue for practitioners who are more interested in developing a competitive sport than adhering to a specific historical swordsmanship style (if it works in freeplay, do it!). For others, the historicity of the actions being performed is *the* most important thing (if it is documented, do it!). My personal preference is for the latter. I did plenty of sport fencing when I was a teenager, but what gets me going now is the idea that what we are doing is as purely historical as possible. This is because I find training for mortal combat to be far more conducive to personal growth than training for tournaments.

This can lead us into a learning problem. It is much easier to learn physical skills when they can be executed live, in their proper context. This of course would lead to injuries and death if we simply applied natural actions without control when studying fencing. Historical swordsmanship methods tend to be *natural actions ordered into a system.* So for example, nine out of ten people if given a sword and asked to hit something with it will perform some kind of forehand descending blow. Depending on how they do it, it may look like something from Fiore, or from the Liechtenauer system, or from some other system that uses downwards blows. It is necessary for us to have a clear idea then of *why* we have a specific preference for one way of doing something over another. Purists may treat this as a purely aesthetic matter: *I prefer it to look like the book*. Pragmatists may treat this as a set of specific compromises inherent in Fiore's way of doing it: *I prefer it to have this specific set of offensive and defensive characteristics.*

Both are useful, and both have their pitfalls. Mindless copying of choreography does not make for the Art of Arms; purely pragmatic adjustments might lead us away from one style and into another (probably better adapted for our freeplay context). So, it is necessary to have a profound awareness of the offensive and defensive compromises being made by specific mechanical choices, and it is similarly necessary to keep in mind the preferred tactical and mechanical choices that make this the art of a specific master.

In my experience the different historical longsword arts for which we have sufficient sources are all effective. Likewise, two students training in the same interpretation of the same art will express that art differently. But it should be clear when watching a practitioner fencing which system he or she is trying to express.

Doctrine, Strategy and Tactics[17]

Every martial art, from *T'ai Chi Chuan* to the nuclear deterrent, is based on a doctrine—an idea of how combat works. The actions and tactics of a given art reflect the conscious and unconscious assumptions of its founder. If we compare two combat sports, boxing and Greco-Roman wrestling, we can see a basically similar situation: two antagonists, without weapons, in a controlled environment, with a specified fighting area and a referee. But they are acting in completely different ways. One pair punches each other, the other rolls around on the ground. In both cases, if the fighters switched tactics, they would be barred from competition. The source of these different approaches is in the minds of the founders of the sports—what constitutes the best way for two fighters to

---

17 For an in-depth discussion of doctrine, strategy and tactics, see Forrest E. Morgan, *Living the Martial Way.*

determine who is better? The rules of the contest are then developed to encourage the desired fighting behaviour, and the techniques most likely to achieve victory are then determined by those rules. So, to contrast these sports, we have:

	Wrestling	Boxing
Doctrine:	Grapples and throws are best	Hitting with hands is best
Strategy	Immobilise opponent	Damage opponent with punches
Tactics	Choose best throws and locks	Multiple combinations of strikes

There is no way to say which is better; both work well in their contexts. But which is better for you? Much depends on your nature, and your body type. This process is exactly the same in a lethal environment. There is no one "best" way for a gun to be carried—or even one "best" gun to carry. So what then is Fiore's doctrine, through what strategy does he apply it, and what tactics result? He does not say directly, so let us work backwards from technique to tactics, from tactics to strategy, from strategy to doctrine.

There are 70 illustrated plays of the sword on foot (including armoured combat). Of these, 35 are explicitly defences, in which the person doing the play has parried an attack. Five require the person doing them to have attacked. The remaining 30 plays follow on from a specific crossing without saying how we got there—it is reasonable to conclude that an attack has been parried, but without creating a clear opportunity for the defender to strike. So, the majority of techniques shown are defences against attacks. In almost every case, the attack is parried first, and then a riposte (a strike made by the defender after a successful parry) of some description follows. This may imply a preference for defensive play. It certainly implies a skilled opponent against whom you must defend yourself. In every case, the attacker's weapon is controlled before we commit to a counter-strike. Even when attacking, we must do so in such a way that we can predict the movement of our opponent's weapon and thus control it. This leads to a lot of grappling, even with the swords in hand.

Yet at the same time Fiore states (in the Pisani-Dossi) that boldness is the key virtue a swordsman must posses, which surely implies a willingness to attack. The overall goals of the combat are: to survive the fight and to gain renown. This is best achieved by striking down the opponent without taking so much as a scratch. Hence a defensively oriented style, executed boldly—running away might work for survival but would certainly diminish the fighter's reputation!

- Tactics: parry and riposte; counterattack; attack. If you are parried, strike on the other side. If attacked, counterattack if able, parry if not. If counterattacked, parry. Execute the most efficient technique from the crossing that results.
- Strategy: control his sword with your sword or a grapple, and strike.
- Doctrine when using a sword out of armour: same as overall doctrine, but assume "sword strikes are best".
- Overall Doctrine: boldness, strength, speed and foresight. Control opponent's weapon and strike.

Finally:

In a nutshell, the Art of Swordsmanship is this:

Identify your offensive and defensive arms. Let's call the thing you defend with "shield", and the thing you hit with, "sword".
Then:

1. Put your shield in the way of his sword.
2. Then hit him with your sword.
3. If his shield is in the way, go around it.
4. Do it all with the shortest possible movement.

That's it. Twenty years of swordsmanship experience reduced to four basic instructions. Got it?
Now go do it.

Chapter Twelve

A FINAL SUMMARY: THE SYSTEM BY NUMBERS

There is a huge amount of material to remember and make use of. It took me 15 years of study and training to have a solid recall of the main points of the system: to be able to put any fencing occurrence into a Fiore context. This section is where you come if you want to know what I have to say about a specific concept, guard, action or play, without wading through the entire book to find it.

This material can be organised any number of ways, but most of it is presented by Fiore in specific groups, so I've arranged it according to the sizes of those groups.

Pairs

Zogho largo, zogho stretto p. 43
Pressure on the blade: strong or weak p. 181
Defences against the thrust: *scambiare di punta* p. 111 and *rompere di punta* p. 108
Lines: inside, outside p. 39

Threes

Parts of the blade: *tutta spada, mezza spada, punta di spada* p. 40
Turns: *volta stabile, mezza volta, tutta volta* p. 60
Three ways to start a drill: attacker moves first, defender moves first, they both move. p. 185

Fours

Four unarmed poste: *longa, zenghiaro, porta di ferro, frontale.* p. 67

Four "things in the art", steps: *accrescere, discressere, passare, tornare* p. 53

Four virtues: *avvisamento, audatia, presteza, forteza* p. 46

Four aspects of any action: time, measure, structure, flow p. 34

Four surviving manuscripts: Getty, Pisani-Dossi, Morgan and BnF p. 5

Four things that can happen as a thrust is parried: feint, strike, yield or wait p. 189

Four drills p. 182

Four Crossings drill p. 184

Four Corners drill p. 183

Fives

Five different thrusts: *mandritto* and *roverso* from above, *mandritto* and *roverso* from below, and up the middle p. 116

Sixes

Six ways of holding the sword p. 140

Six things that can happen as a cut is parried: strike, feint, bind, angulate, yield or wait p. 189

Sevens

Seven blows: Fiore names eleven blows of the sword, but refers to them as a group of seven: *mandritto fendente, roverso fendente, mandritto sottano, roverso sottano, mandritto mezano, roverso mezano,* the thrust (*punta*) p. 116

Seven crossings drill. p. 184

Eights

The eight things you need in *abrazare* (wrestling) are: strength, speed, knowledge of grips, knowledge of how to break limbs, knowledge of how to apply joint locks (*ligadure*, binds), knowledge of where to strike (the "places of pain"!), knowledge of how to throw your opponent to the ground, knowledge of how to dislocate limbs. p. 45

First eight plays of the dagger (disarm, counter, lock, counter, break, counter, takedown): pp. 49–67, *The Medieval Dagger.*

Twelves

Twelve guards of the longsword in two hands: *posta di tutta porta di ferro* p. 87, *posta di donna destra* p. 84, *posta di fenestra* p. 104, *posta di donna la sinestra* p. 86, *posta longa* p. 89, *mezana porta di ferro* p. 101, *posta breve* p. 120, *posta di dente di zenghiaro* p. 88, *posta di bicorno* p. 122, *posta di coda longa* p. 90, *posta frontale* p. 96, *posta di dente di zenghiaro la mezana* p. 88

Note that you could rearrange this as a group of ten if you like, by omitting the repeated guards (*donna* on the left, *zenghiaro*), or nine if you also leave out one of the *porta di ferro* guards.

Twelve plays of the sword in one hand, if we included the master, p. 147

Using the Segno

Fiore, in his infinite wisdom and compassion, also provides a map upon which we can mark our particular route through this maze. The *segno* page is built to store groups of seven and four especially easily, and is also easily adapted for threes, fives and twelves. In both the Pisani- Dossi MS and the BnF the swords illustrate the same angles as the blows (which is not true in the Getty) and the segno comes with nine guards added, written in the spaces around the swords (it's missing *frontale* and *bicorno*). I suggest printing out a copy and annotating it according to your own needs and interests.

Appendix A

Warming Up

The warm-up is a very important part of a training session. It helps to develop your strength and fitness, forms a segue from normal life to training, and helps prevent injuries. Most importantly, it allows you to focus on the hardware (your body) upon which you are about to run the software program (Fiore 1.1). If you are generally fit and in tune with your body, then you may not need a warm-up at all, but for most students it is very helpful.

A properly constructed warm-up involves three things: loosening the joints, warming the body, and light stretching. Ideally it will also activate core stabiliser muscles, increase strength, and increase both aerobic and anaerobic endurance. There is a vast array of potential warm-up exercises, and I encourage my students to play around with what works for them. If you have your own routines from other activities, feel free to use them. This section is intended for those for whom this is their first and only physical practice. Have a go at every exercise here, at least in its most basic form, and once you have an idea of what is involved, pick and choose from each group depending on how you feel on any given day.

Loosening Up

1. Swinging: Feet wide apart, weight on one bent leg, arms totally relaxed, push across from one leg to the other, bending the knee and turning your hips and shoulders. The arms swing naturally. Keep your back upright, head up, and let the motion of your arms be driven only by your legs. You will feel your back twisting gently, stretching the muscles around your spine (GENTLY!). Pay attention to how your body feels, and repeat

this exercise at the end of the warm-up to see how effective the warm-up has been. With practice, how this swinging feels at the beginning tells you exactly what to emphasise in the rest of the warm-up session.

2. Knee rotations: begin with your feet quite close together. Place your hands on your knees. Gently turn your knees 15 times clockwise then anticlockwise. Then open your knees turning them in opposite directions, 15 times each way.

3. Hip rotations: hands on hips, feet shoulder- width apart. Rotate the hips 20 times anticlockwise, then reverse. This should be done with bent knees, and the lower back should be doing practically all the work.

4. Back rotations: widen your stance, reach up to the sky with both hands, then, keeping the legs slightly bent, but not flexing them, rotate the whole body nine times each way, describing as large a circle as possible with your hands. The centre of rotation is the hips and lower back. Change direction when the hands are by the floor, and finish in that position.

5. Arm rotations: keeping the arms relaxed and straight (but without locking the elbows), swing them from the shoulders 12 times around backwards, then 12 times forward, then 12 times right arm forward, left arm backwards, then reverse.

6. Open chest: cross your arms loosely over your chest, then swing them horizontally backwards, then back across, 12 times. Alternate so that the right hand crosses above then below the left.

7. Wrist rolls: curl your fingers towards the inside of your wrist then extend them out, as if picking lint off your cuffs and flicking it away.

8. Neck rotations: turn your head clockwise six times, then the other way. Do not tip the head back. Make the circles just large enough to feel a slight stretch in the muscles.

9. Neck turns: Look over your right shoulder, then your left, in turn. Six times each side.

10. Neck tips: look up at the sky, then down at the floor, stretching in turn your throat and your neck. Six times.
11. Neck tilts: tilt your head to one side then the other, as if to lay your ear on your shoulder. Keep your shoulders down. Six times.

Warming the Body

1. Scoops: with your feet wide apart, place your hands on the floor shoulder-width apart and walk them forwards, leaving your feet where they are. You should now be in a press-up position, but with your legs spread and your hips in the air. Rock your weight back onto your feet, leaving your hands where they are. From here, breathing in, scoop down towards the floor, bending the arms, then swoop up, with your head up, back bent backwards, hips near the floor, arms and legs straight. Breathing out, reverse the motion so the weight returns to the feet and your hips rise up. Beginners may find doing just one of these very difficult. Aim to build up your strength over many months, eventually you should be able to do at least 20.
2. Ski-running: stand left foot and right arm forward, left arm and right foot back. Keeping your feet parallel, and swinging your arms back and forth in time to your feet, "ski" on the spot with as much length and smoothness as possible. 25 repetitions should get the blood moving.
3. Star jumps (aka jumping jacks): standing with feet together and hands by your sides, swiftly touch your hands together above your head and open your legs wide. Immediately return to the start position. Repeat 25 times.
4. Squats: start with your feet parallel and about shoulder width apart, arms out in front of you. Swing your arms back and drop into a squat, keeping your knees pointed in the direction of your feet. Keep your body upright. Hips towards feet, not face towards floor. In one smooth action swing your arms forwards and stand up. About 20 makes a nice gentle leg warm-up.

5. Push-ups: the standard push-up goes like this: start with your feet together, hands shoulder- width apart on the floor, body straight, shoulders, hips and heels in one straight line. Keeping everything else the same, bend your arms until your lowest point is half an inch off the ground, then push back up. If one is a challenge, build up slowly. Aim for at least 20 being an easy part of a warm-up. Refer to *The Little Book of Push-ups* for useful and enjoyable variations, and training guidelines.

6. Starfish: lie on your back, arms and legs wide. Smoothly place your left hand on your right foot (which remains on the floor). Roll back along your right side and smoothly up and place your right hand on your left foot. Repeat each way five times. A smooth rolling motion is ideal. Your spine should not grind on the floor.

Stabiliser Exercises:

1. The Plank: lie on the floor, face down with your elbows under you; feet together, toes digging in. Gather your waist, chest and legs into a straight line. Lift yourself up, keeping your back flat and your body in a straight line, hold for about 30 seconds. Build up until 60 seconds is no challenge.

2. Killer plank: assume plank position, hold for 30 seconds; lift and extend right foot, hold for 15 seconds; switch feet, left foot extended, hold for 15 seconds; both feet down, lift left arm to chest, shoulders remain parallel with the ground, hold for 15 seconds; switch arms, right arm off, hold for 15 seconds; return to start position, hold for 30 seconds (total, 2 minutes).

3. Whisky and cigars: essential for any good training regime ... sit on the floor, legs straight, back straight. Imagine you are in an armchair, and put your feet up on an imaginary silk footstool. Both legs come completely off the floor—only your buttocks remain in contact. Reach behind you to the right for your whisky (single malt, of course), and to the left for a good, hand-rolled (imaginary) cigar.

You should now be reasonably warmed up, with the major joints active and supple. If you feel any particularly stiff bits, loosen those up before stretching.

Stretches

Stretching in a warm-up is all about finding the normal range of motion for a joint, and nothing at all to do with flexibility. For flexibility training, stretches need to be done isometrically, or held for at least 30 seconds or so. Both of these approaches increase range by resetting the stretch reflex, but both come with the price of temporarily weakening the muscle, making it more prone to injury.

Warm-up stretches should be held for less than 10 seconds, and are mainly diagnostic—can my body move as far as it should, or am I still tight from sitting at a computer all day? Tightness should be cured with exercise, not stretching.

1. Stand straight, feet together, and reach up as high as you can. Then keeping the legs straight, bend down as far as is comfortable, centring the movement in your hips. You will feel this stretch in the backs of your legs or in your spine. It doesn't matter: the stiffest part will be getting stretched. Hold for 5-10 seconds, then slowly return to an upright position, starting at your tailbone and rolling the spine up, head last.
2. Repeat the above exercise, but first cross one leg over the other, feet together and pointing forwards. This focuses the stretch in the back of the rear leg. Hold for 5-10 seconds, then rise up and change the feet over, and repeat.
3. Inside stretch: open the legs, keeping the feet parallel, as far as is comfortable, then sink down onto one foot, keeping both feet flat on the ground, and your extended leg straight. This stretches the inside of the extended leg. Hold for 5-10 seconds, then change sides.
4. Lunge stretch: turn one foot out so that it is at right angles

to the other. Step out, bending the knee, sinking almost all of your weight to one foot. Keep your back straight, and the rear leg extended. Both feet are flat on the floor, and the bent front knee remains directly above the ankle. Try to keep your pelvis in line with your front thigh. Hands can go on your hips. Hold for 5-10 seconds, then change sides.

5.   Toe-up: feet parallel and wide apart, shift the weight to one foot, sinking as low as possible. Allow the unweighted foot to turn up, toes pointing to the ceiling. If this does not stretch you, lean down and reach with your hands for the upright foot. Hold for 5-10 seconds, then change sides. Keep the heel of the supporting foot on the ground. It doesn't matter if you can't go very low. Keep your hands off the floor. This is also a balance exercise.

6.   Heel-up: return to the lunge position, and turn your hips forward, allowing the back heel to rise, dropping and flexing the rear knee. You should feel this in the front of the rear thigh. Hold for 5-10 seconds, then change sides.

7.   Shoulder stretch: reach up behind your back with your left hand, reach over your right shoulder with your right hand, and link hands between your shoulder blades. If you can't manage this straight away, use a stick, a towel or something similar to connect your hands. Hold for 5-10 seconds, then change sides. You can place the stretch in the tricep of the upper arm or the deltoids of the lower arm.

8.   Extend your left hand in front of you, palm up, thumb pointed to the left. Place your right hand underneath it, also palm up, and grasp your left thumb with your right fingers. Use your right hand to twist your left arm anticlockwise, keeping the elbow straight. Hold for 5-10 seconds, then change sides.

9.   Extend your left hand in front of you, palm down, thumb pointed to the right. Place your right hand on top, and hook your right thumb over the little-finger edge of your left hand.

Use your right hand to twist your left arm clockwise, keeping the elbow straight. Hold for 5-10 seconds, then change sides.

After stretching your wrists and arms, shake out your arms, clench and unclench your fists a few times, checking for sore spots. These warm-up exercises and stretches are not specific to Western swordsmanship, neither are they an exhaustive list. Feel free to import any warm-up exercises from other martial arts or sports that you have found work for you. Every body is different; try to find the combination of exercises and stretches that suits yours the best. Remember to breathe deeply and easily throughout the warm-up, and be gentle with the stretches. It is also important to move smoothly from one position to the next. This warm-up should leave you feeling warm, loose, and relaxed. Pick enough exercises that it takes about 12-15 minutes, for a gentle warm-up—but feel free to include more of the aerobic and stabiliser exercises for a conditioning workout.

Conditioning exercises and guidelines can be found at http://www.swordschool.com/wiki/index.php/ Conditioning.

APPENDIX B

Glossary

This is a list of terms from Fiore's treatise and from standard modern fencing usage that are commonly used in training. The translations offered are specific to this treatise, and are not necessarily applicable to modern Italian or other historical sources. Students should also note that the terms are often spelled several different ways in the original sources. Those interested in the translation process should read my article "Half Full? Translating *Mezza* and *Tutta* in *Il Fior di Battaglia*" available free online.

Italian grammar is quite simple, but has some aspects that English speakers may find odd—not least that a single word may have different forms, and to make a word plural, we can't just throw an 's' on the end. In general, nouns are either masculine or feminine, and adjectives will have both masculine and feminine forms that agree with the noun they describe. For example: punt*a* fals*a*, false thrust. Fil*o* fals*o*, false edge. In general:

- Nouns ending in -e when singular will end in -i when plural: fendent*e*, fendent*i*.
- Nouns ending in -o when singular will end in -i when plural: colp*o*, colp*i*.
- Nouns ending in -a when singular will end in -e when plural: ligadur*a*, ligadur*e*.

While it is standard practice to place all adjectives in their masculine form first, in the list below I have placed each word in the form that is most commonly used in Fiore (e.g. *Longa*), and used the spellings that you will find in this book and in Fiore's (*zogho*,

212

for example, would be *gioco* in modern Italian). These terms are frequently combined: for example, *mandritto fendente* is a forehand descending blow.

Abrazare: to wrestle.
Accrescere: a step forwards without passing. Alla traversa: diagonally across.
Attack: the first offensive movement.
Bicorno: two-horned. Specifically a guard position.
Breve: short. Specifically a guard position.
Colpo (plural: colpi): a blow, either cut or thrust.
Counterattack: an offensive movement (cut or thrust) used to counter an attack by defending and striking in one motion.
Destro: on the right.
Discrescere (noun: discrescimento): to step back without passing.
Donna: lady. Specifically a guard position.
Falso: false.
Fendente: a descending blow.
Fenestra: window. Specifically a guard position.
Fora di strada: out of the way or off the line; as in "accresco fora distrada", "I step off the line".
Frontale: frontal. Specifically a guard position.
Ligadura: a lock. Ligadura soprana = high lock; ligadura mezana = middle lock; ligadura sottana = lower lock.
Longa: long. Specifically a guard position. Mandritto: forehand.
Mezza/mezana: middle or half, depending on context.
Mezano: one of the six cuts, these are horizontal. Literally, "middle blow".
Parry: a successful deflection of any offensive movement.
Passare: to pass; to step passing one foot past the other.
Passo: a passing step; also the space between your feet. Hence *passo alla traversa* = pass across. Porta di ferro: iron door. Specifically a guard position, either middle (*mezana*) or whole (*tutta*).

214 ◆ APPENDIX B

Posta: Guard position. Plural *poste*. Punta: point (of a weapon), or a thrust.

Rebattere: to beat aside, specifically an incoming weapon.

Remedio: remedy; specifically the defence against an attack, usually some form of parry.

Riposte: the offensive action done by the defender immediately following his successful parry.

Rompere: to break, as in *rompere di punta*, to break the thrust (a defensive action).

Roverso: backhand.

Scambiare: to exchange. Specifically, *scambiare di punta*, the exchange of thrust (a defensive action).

Sinestra: on the left.

Sottano: a rising blow.

Strada: way, line. Specifically the line between two fencers. Usually in context *fora di strada*, off the line.

Tondo: a horizontal blow (as *mezano*).

Tornare: to pass backwards.

Tutta: whole or full.

Vera croce: true cross. Specifically a guard position.

Volta: turn, specifically *volta stabile*, stable turn; *mezza volta*, half turn; *tutta volta*, whole turn.

Zenghiaro: wild boar. Specifically a guard position. Usual form *"posta di dente di zenghiaro"*, position of the wild boar's tooth.

Zogho largo: wide play. Specifically actions with weapons that occur before a crossing is made or after a crossing in which the points are wide.

Zogho stretto: close play. Specifically actions that occur after a crossing is made with the points in presence and some pressure in the bind.

Acknowledgements

This book is the culmination of many years of research and training, with input of some kind from almost everyone I've crossed swords with in that time, at home and abroad. At home, I could point to specific aspects of interpretation that are directly due to the insight of my students, especially Ilkka Hartikainen, Mikko Hänninen, Christopher Blakey, Kenneth Quek, Topi Mikkola, Jan Kukkamäki, and Pirkka Palmio. The willingness of my students to tell me they disagree and point to the page in Fiore they think I've misread has been absolutely crucial to the development of my understanding of this Art. Abroad, thanks are especially due to my colleagues and friends Tom Leoni, Greg Mele, Sean Hayes, Rob Lovett and Christian Tobler, none of whom just take my word for any point of research, but insist on evidence and a reasonable argument.

Jari Juslin took the 1500 photographs from which the 300 or so here were culled, and did the endless processing to bring them to a pitch of perfection never before seen in a martial arts book.

Greg Mele and Tom Leoni both put in a lot of editing work, making major improvements (and suggesting splitting the magnum opus into several books). This book is much better for their efforts.

Eric Artzt worked through the manuscript sword in hand, spotting errors and making suggestions that have dramatically improved this book.

Two of the best novelists alive today happen to be also longsword enthusiasts, and served as test readers: Neal Stephenson and Christian Cameron. You may imagine what it feels like to have such writers critiquing my work.

Bob Charron gave two seminars at my school, in 2003 and 2005, which significantly improved my grasp of the system, and helped lay the foundation for much of my later work.

My first fencing coaches, Gail and Alan Rudge and Prof Bert Bracewell, nurtured my love of the sword.

Prof Philip Bruce's courses on how to teach fencing skills have made me a much better teacher.

My T'ai Chi teacher Steve Fox taught me structure and flow.

My agent, Shelley Power, took me on largely on faith. I hope to live up to it.

My sister, Claire Bodanis, took my polished, perfect, final, draft and found approximately 500 typos and other errors in it.

My student Kliment Yanev, did a thorough editing pass and corrected dozens of typos, and made some excellent usability suggestions. The inestimable Bek Pickard of Zebedee Design, for making the book beautiful.

My long-suffering students gave up their weekends for the photo-shoots, and patiently endured reshoots, technical problems, and my endless fiddling with their positions: Mikko Hänninen, Julia Arkanova, Jukka Salmi, Juhani Nissilä, Auri Poso, Joni Karjalainen, Ville Kastari, Jan Kukkamäki and Kenneth Quek.

Writing a book takes its toll on the whole family, so let me acknowledge here the forgiving natures of my wife Michaela, and my daughters Grace and Katriina.

To all of the above, many thanks!

INDIEGOGO CAMPAIGN CONTRIBUTORS

As with *Veni VADI Vici*, and the *Audatia* game, the funds to lay out and produce this book came from a legion of bold supporters, who bought copies in advance through my crowd-funding campaign. You can see the campaign page here: http://igg.me/at/longsword.

Some chose to remain anonymous, the rest are named below. Thank you all for believing in my work!

Aaron Glimme

Aaron Jones

Adam Surber

Alberto Dainese

Aleksi Airaksinen

Alex Clark

Alexander Foster

Alexander Hollinger

Alexander Sandosham

Allan Stevns

Anders Malmsten

Andrea Morini

Andreas Kammel

Andrew Gilmartin

Andrew J Lackovic

Andrew Malloy

Andrew Mizener

Andrew Moore

Andrew Rozycki

Andrew Somlyo

Andrew South

Andrzej Kuszell

Andy Gibson

Andy Groom

Anette Säkö

Anthony Hurst

Antti Jauhiainen

Arnar Hafsteinsson

Artis Aboltins

Arttu Junnila

Arturo Banda

Ashe Richards

Bastian Busch-Garbe

Ben Holman

Ben Schreiber

Benjamin Ford

Benjamin House

Benjamin Szymanel

Benjamin Vonarx
bidoof
Bittmann, G.
Brian Stewart
Brian W Batronis
Bruce Harlick
Carey Martell
Carter Bush
Cathy Spencer
Cay Blomqvist
Cecilia Äijälä
Charles Deily
Charles Taylor
Charlotte Villa
Chris Bartus
Chris Hare
Chris Lauricella
Christian Engelund
Christoph Busche
Christopher Cooke
Christopher Halpin-Durband
Claire Bodanis
Cody Hartley
Cody Kerr
Culann Farrell
Daniel Blay
Daniel Cadenbach
Daniel Gerszewski
Darko Andreas Zuercher
Dave Kroncke
Dave Wayne
David Britten
David Empey
David Harrison

David Rudd
Dawfydd Kelly
Denís Fernández Cabrera
Dierk Hagedorn
Dietrich Dellinger
Doug Hulick
Dougg Joness
Elizabeth Beyreis
Eneko Villanueva Verdejo
Eoin Brennan
Eric Artzt
Erica Stark
Erik White
Ernesto Maldonado
Evan Ringo
Federico Dall'Olio
Federico Griggio
Florian Cesic
Franklin Walther
Garrett Harper
Gemac – Esgrima Medieval – Porto
George Lewis
Gindi Wauchope
Görner, Michael
Grégoire Dubois
Haris Dimitriou
Harry den Ouden
Heikki Hallamaa
Henry Vilhunen
Ian Tustin
Ilpo Luhtala
Ioannis Papadopoulos
Irene Amoruso

Jaakko Tahkokallio
James Fisher
James Piesse
James Wran
Jan Kukkamaki
Jan Stals
Janne Hurskainen
Jarkko Hietaniemi
Jason McBrayer
Javier Andrés Chamorro Bernal
Jean-Rémy Gallapont
Jeffry Larson
Jennifer L Corrigan
Jennifer Landels
Jeremy Bornstein
Jeremy Coyle
Jeremy Tavan
Jessica Burley
Jim Steiner
Joakim Westerberg
Joel Norman
Johanus Haidner
John McLaughlin
John Patterson
John Rothe
John Sugden
John Van Lennep
Jonas Schiött
Jonathan Besler
Joni Karjalainen
Joonas Iivonen
Joonas Lahtiharju
Jouni Alanärä
Juhani Gradistanac

Juho Hännikäinen
Jukka Heinänen
Jukka Varjovuori
Jussi Hytönen
Jussi Laasonen
Justin Snyder
Justin Weaver
Juuso Koivunen
Karin Levenstein
Kary "Realm Master K" Williams
Katrin Wendland
Keith Nelson
Kenric Lee
Kevin Inouye
Kevin Murakoshi
Kevin O'Brien
Kliment Yanev
Konstantin Tsvetkov
Lars Olsen
Lesley Mitchell
Lloyd Eldred
Lorna Winn
Louise Mann
Lukas Lehmann
Luke Ireland
Mackenzie Cosens
Marc Auger
Marco A Assfalk de Oliveira
Marcus Vencel
Mark Allen
Mark Bottomley
Mark Cogan
Mark Davidson
Mark Jolliff

Mark Nelson
Mark Teppo
Markku Mulari
Markku Rontu
Marko Saari
Markus Schoenlau
Martin Noack
Martin Sanders
Martin Wilkinson
Mathieu Glachant
Matthew Mole
Matthew Schmid
Matthew Stewart-Fulton
Merja Polvinen
Michael Baker
Michael Jarvis
Michael Payne
Michael Prendergast
Michael T. Stokes
Michal Barcikowski
Mikko Behm
Mikko Hänninen
Mikko Korhonen
Mikko Parviainen
Mikko Sillanpää
Mira Aaltio
N. Eddiford
Neal Stephenson
Neil Muller
Neufeld Tamás
Nicholas Barton
Nico Möller
Niko Tanhuanpää
Nikodemus Siivola

Noah Bacon
Noora Kumpulainen
Nuutti Vertanen
Olli-Pekka Korpela
Otto Kopra
Oula Kitti
Patrick Shirley
Patrik Olterman
Paul Mullins
Paul Wagner
Perttu Hämäläinen
Peter Törlind
Petri Ihatsu
Petri Wessman
Philip Kramm
Philipp Jaindl
Phillip Pierce-Savoie
Phoebus Ferratus
Pier Antonio Bianchi
Ralph Hempel
Ralph Miller
Rami Laaksonen
Randy Holte
René Kriek
Richard Crabtree
Richard Cullinan
Richard Jurgens
Richard Lowry
Robert Charrette
Robert Fisher
Robert Mauler
Robert Sayers
Robert Sulentic
Robin D. Toll

Roger Svalberg
Roland Cooper
Roland Fuhrmann
Ronny Kilén
Royce Calverley
Ryan Wolf
Samuel Munilla
Scott Aldinger
Scott Nimmo
Sean Hastings
Sébastien Jubeau
Sergei Terjajev
Shannon Walker
Simone Zarbin
Stacy Stocki
Stefano Salvadori
Stephen Hobson
Steve Planchin
Steven Danielson
Susanna Sorvali
Suvi Ylioja
Szymon Szymanski
Taneli Pirinen
Tapio Pellinen
Teemu Kari
Tero Alanko
Terry Olson
Thomas Belloma
Thomas Griffiths
Tia Kiesiläinen
Tiago Ferreira
Tim Owens
Tim Trant

Timon Pike
Timothy Carroll
Tina Aspiala
Titta Tolvanen
Tom Hudson
Tom McKinnell
Tomas Suazo
Tome Loh
Tony C Nelson
Tony Stewart
Topi Mikkola
Tracy Mellow
Tuomas Lempiäinen
Tuomo Aimonen
Tuukka Pääkkönen
Tuuli Salmi
Valeri Saltikoff
Ville Henell
Ville Kankainen
Ville Kastari
Ville Vihikangas
Ville Vuorela
Ville-Hermanni Kilpiä
Walter Neubauer
Walter Vasquez
Warhorse Studios
Wesley Arnold
William Brickman
Wolfgang Pretl
Yancy Orchard
Younghwan Choo
Zoë Chandler

BIBLIOGRAPHY

Primary Sources:

Il Fior di Battaglia (MS Ludwig XV13), J. P. Getty museum in Los Angeles.

Il Fior di battaglia di Fiore dei Liberi da Cividale (Il Codice Ludwig XV 13 del J. Paul Getty Museum), Massimo Malipiero, 2006

Fiore de' Liberi's Fior di Battaglia translation into English by Tom Leoni, 2009

Flos Duellatorum, in private hands in Italy, but published in facsimile in 1902 by Francesco Novati.

Il Fior di Battaglia Morgan MS M 383, Pierpont Morgan museum, New York

Florius de Arte Luctandi (MS. LATIN 11269), Bibliotheque Nationale Francaise in Paris

De Arte Gladiatoria Dimicandi, Filippo Vadi, translated by Luca Porzio and Gregory Mele, 2002

Dell'arte di Scrimia, Giovanni Dall' Agocchie, 1572

Gran Simulacro del arte e del uso della scherma, Ridolfo Capoferro, 1610

Secondary Sources:

The Inner Game of Tennis, W. Timothy Gallwey, 1974

Meditations on Violence, Sgt Rory Miller, 2008

On Killing, Lt. Col. Dave Grossman, 1996 *The Art of Learning,* Josh Waitzkin, 2008 *The Living Sword*, Aldo Nadi, 1995

The Unconquered Knight: the Chronicle of Pero Niño, Gutierre Diaz de Gamez, tr. Joan Evans, 2004

Knightly Art of the Longsword, David Lindholm, 2003

Further reading from the same author
If you've enjoyed this book, you might like my blog (guywindsor. net/blog). And please consider buying one or more of the following:

The Swordsman's Companion, a training manual for medieval longsword, 2004

The Duellist's Companion, a training manual for 17th century Italian rapier, 2006

The Little Book of Push-ups, 2009: the title says it all.

The Armizare Vade Mecum, mnemonic verses for remembering Fiore's Art. 2011

Mastering the Art of Arms vol 1: The Medieval Dagger, a training manual for Fiore's dagger material. 2012

Veni VADI Vici, a transcription and translation of Filippo Vadi's *De Arte Gladiatoria Dimicandi*, with commentary and analysis. 2013.

Mastering the Art of Arms, vol 3: Longsword, Advanced Techniques and Concepts (forthcoming in 2016).

Swordfighting, for Writers, Game Designers and Martial Artists (forthcoming in 2014)

If you already have them all, thank you for your generous support of my work!

Finally, let me ask you now to review this book, for better or worse, wherever is convenient for you. If I've done something right, I need to know to do it again; and still more I need to know what could be improved. As Vadi wrote: "And if this my little work finds its way into the hands of anyone versed in the art and appears to him to have anything superfluous or wrong, please adjust, reduce or add to it as he pleases. Because in the end I place myself under his correction and censure." Thank you!

ABOUT THE AUTHOR

Guy Windsor has been researching historical Italian swordsmanship and knightly combat since the late nineties, and has been teaching the Art of Arms professionally since 2001. His books include *The Swordsman's Companion, The Duellist's Companion, Veni Vadi Vici,* and the *Mastering the Art of Arms* series. He also blogs on swordsmanship at guywindsor.net/blog

He lives in Helsinki, Finland, with his wife and daughters.

www.swordschool.com

Lightning Source UK Ltd.
Milton Keynes UK
UKOW05f1936170317
296936UK00003B/55/P

9 789526 819327